CW00833422

PATRIARCHY

Patriarchy, particularly as embedded in the Old and New Testaments and Roman legal precepts, has been a powerful organising concept with which social order has been understood, maintained, enforced, contested, adjudicated and dreamt about for over two millennia of Western history. This brief book surveys three influential episodes in this history: seventeenth-century debates about absolutism and democracy, nineteenth-century reconstructions of human prehistory, and the broad mobilisations linked to twentieth-century women's movements. It then looks at the way feminist scholars have reconsidered and revised some earlier explanations built around patriarchy. The book concludes with an overview of current uses of the concept of patriarchy – from fundamentalist Christian activism, over foreign policy analyses of oppressive regimes, to scholarly debates about forms of effective governance. By treating patriarchy as a powerful tool to think with, rather than a factual description of social relations, the text makes a useful contribution to current social and political thought.

Pavla Miller is Professor of Historical Sociology in the School of Global, Urban and Social Studies at the Royal Melbourne Institute of Technology (Australia).

KEY IDEAS
Series Editor: Peter Hamilton

Designed to compliment the successful *Key Sociologists*, this series covers the main concepts, issues, debates and controversies in sociology and the social sciences. The series aims to provide authoritative essays on central topics of social science, such as community, power, work, sexuality, inequality, benefits and ideology, class, family, etc. Books adopt a strong 'individual' line, as critical essays rather than literature surveys, offering lively and original treatments of their subject matter. The books will be useful to students and teachers of sociology, political science, economics, psychology, philosophy and geography.

For more information please visit: www.routledge.com/Key-Ideas/book-series/SE0058.

Recent books in the series:

PATRIARCHY

Pavla Miller

Routledge
Taylor & Francis Group

LONDON AND NEW YORK

First published 2017
by Routledge
2 Park Square, Milton Park, Abingdon, Oxon OX14 4RN

and by Routledge
711 Third Avenue, New York, NY 10017

Routledge is an imprint of the Taylor & Francis Group, an informa business

British Library Cataloguing in Publication Data
A catalogue record for this book is available from the British Library

Library of Congress Cataloging in Publication Data
Names: Miller, Pavla, 1950- author.
Title: Patriarchy / by Pavla Miller.
Description: Milton Park, Abingdon, Oxon ; New York, NY : Routledge, [2017]
Identifiers: LCCN 2016057653| ISBN 9781138692435 (hardback) | ISBN 9781138692442 (pbk.) | ISBN 9781315532370 (ebook)
Subjects: LCSH: Patriarchy.
Classification: LCC GN479.6 .M55 2017 | DDC 321/.1–dc23
LC record available at https://lccn.loc.gov/2016057653

ISBN: 978-1-138-69243-5 (hbk)
ISBN: 978-1-138-69244-2 (pbk)
ISBN: 978-1-315-53237-0 (ebk)

Typeset in Bembo
by Taylor & Francis Books

Printed and bound by CPI Group (UK) Ltd, Croydon, CR0 4YY

To the memory of Mary-Anne Roberts

CONTENTS

ACKNOWLEDGEMENTS

Many friends, colleagues, students and neighbours contributed to this book. I am grateful to them all. Several deserve particular thanks. Jock McCulloch and his little friend Bernie provided sound scholarly advice and excellent cakes. Des Cahill supplied invaluable advice regarding God and his servants. Julia Adams organised (and her university financed) an invaluable workshop on patrimonialism. Finally, Karen Turner helped make sure the text was accessible.

1

THINKING WITH PATRIARCHY

Most readers opening a book on patriarchy would expect to see a brief overview of the relative position of men and women in society. This would highlight the extent of past and current gender inequalities in different parts of the world, and the extent of violence against women and children. This summary would then be followed by an overview of plausible explanations of this state of affairs, and introduce the concept of patriarchy as a powerful conceptual tool, both for understanding what is going on and attempting to change it. Other readers might expect a thorough feminist critique of just such an approach, pointing out its ethnocentric, historical and theoretical flaws.

This is a different sort of book. It does not try to define what patriarchy really is, or persuade readers to abandon or continue using the concept. Apart from reiterating that the past is extremely complicated, it does not try to provide a systematic overview of how people lived their lives, and women were – and are – systematically oppressed. Rather, the text explores how the term 'patriarchy' has been used and what conceptual work it was expected to perform. It also considers some of the uses, benefits and drawbacks of using the concept of patriarchy to deal with the present. In brief, the book treats patriarchy as a powerful tool to think with, rather than a factual description of social orders.

What inspired this sort of approach? Some years ago, I wrote a long book dealing with historical transformations of one form of patriarchy into another in Western countries (Miller 1998). Throughout, I was vaguely uneasy about not nailing down precisely what patriarchy was. I promised myself that this would be my next project. I then began reading various detailed feminist definitions. These were not just different but often incompatible; feminist theoreticians' valiant attempts to bring them into a coherent system had a lot of merit but finally were not all that convincing. Besides, who was I – or anyone else for that matter – to try and convince millions of feminists everywhere to use a key concept in one particular way?

As I was pondering all this, attempts to construct grand overarching theoretical explanations went out of academic fashion. However, the work of a number of authors suggested an alternative – and exciting – way forward. The ones I liked best combined a robust appreciation of social relations in particular times and places with attention to the development and use of important and powerful conceptual tools (see for example Stoler 1995; Chakrabarty 2000; Ortner 1996; Connell 2011). How can such an approach be applied to patriarchy?

First, people reflect on the world with things which are 'good to think with'.[1] Families are clearly among such concepts; in any case, 'thinking with the family' – often explicitly and literally a *patriarchal* family – crops up again and again in historical and anthropological accounts of the most diverse societies. Second, even though contemporaries tend to regard their own familial arrangements as natural and universal, such conceptual tools are in fact historically situated, and embody quite specific local understandings of kin and household arrangements. As anthropologists keep reminding us, 'in human societies, nothing is nature – but culture makes it so' (cited in Kertzer and Keith 1984: 21). Third, familial metaphors are more than tools for thought; they can be seen both as *constitutive abstractions* guiding practice and as laboratories for working out social categories and boundaries in messy everyday practice.[2] Importantly, some familial metaphors refer to social arrangements existing long before the protagonists' lifetime, yet familiar to them through a thick tapestry of shared understandings. All this gained another dimension in the context of projects 'provincialising' Western social and political thought. As Chakrabarty (2007: 141) explained it:

the so called universal ideas that European thinkers produced in the period from the Renaissance to the Enlightenment and that have since influenced projects of modernity and modernization all over the world, could never be completely universal and pure concepts … For the very language and the circumstances of their formulation must have imported into them intimations of pre-existing histories that were singular and unique, histories that belonged to the multiple pasts of Europe. Irreducible elements of those parochial histories must have lingered into concepts that otherwise seemed to be meant for all. To 'provincialize' Europe was precisely to find out how and in what sense European ideas that were universal were also, at one and the same time, drawn from very particular intellectual and historical traditions that could not claim any universal validity.

These four insights became the core guiding ideas of this book. Patriarchy, I argue, particularly as embedded in the Old and New Testaments in the Bible and in Roman legal precepts, has been a powerful organising concept with which social order has been understood, maintained, enforced, contested, adjudicated and dreamt about for over two millennia of Western history. The concept has been used to tell people dissatisfied with their lives that they should stop complaining and do what they are told, because, as written in the Bible, that is how things have been from time immemorial. In articulating their sense of injustice, groups of peasants, disaffected youth, colonised peoples and women drew on New Testament passages promising equality of all believers. Detailed principles for sorting out the legal rights and duties of patriarchs, as crafted into a logically coherent system by Roman jurists 2,000 years ago and taught to generations of educated men since the 1500s, have been used to adjudicate routine disputes between masters and servants and husbands and wives, and work out who owns what. In recent decades, the same legal precedents have been addressed in working out how to draft legislation criminalising rape in marriage.

The nineteenth-century German philosopher Hegel used ancient Greek tragedies and their depictions of patriarchal powers to articulate what he believed were fundamental tensions between the state and the family; the Austrian physician Freud used the same materials to theorise the workings of the individual psyche. When nineteenth-century 'fathers of social science' tried to make sense of the immense stretch of time that separated early humans from people today, they drew on their classical education to speculate about matriarchal and patriarchal stages of human prehistory. Convinced that the patriarchal family was a key pillar of state oppression, anarchists such as the Russian Michael Bakunin called for its abolition – as did many sections of the radical student movements of the 1960s. In the twentieth century, the concept of patriarchy has been employed as an effective feminist tool to explain the spread and tenacity of women's oppression and to mobilise against injustice – and by anti-feminists to justify and try to resurrect male superiority.

The book deals with three distinct episodes in this long and complicated history: seventeenth-century debates about absolutism and democracy, nineteenth-century reconstructions of human prehistory, and the broad mobilisations linked to twentieth-century women's movements. The text concludes with an overview of current uses of the concept of patriarchy – from fundamentalist Christian activism and everyday feminist texts, over foreign policy analyses of oppressive regimes, to scholarly debates about different forms of governance.

All this might sound like a clever way of not taking sides, and deftly sitting on the fence. But there is also a strong claim here. The way we understand and frame important dimensions of inequality and injustice has important consequences for social action and public policy (Entman 1993; Bacchi 2009). Not only do some of these framings provide more useful toolkits for change, some are experienced as seriously harmful by the very people they are designed to help. Women of colour and underprivileged people from non-Western countries are particularly affected.

Importantly, to be effective, theoretical arguments do not need to be accurate and coherent, and invented traditions do not have to be true. As Craig Calhoun put it, cultural traditions become bases for nationalism – or ethnic identity – when they effectively constitute historical memory, when they inculcate it as 'habitus' or as 'prejudice', not when (or because) their claims relate to an 'accurate' rendering of social history (Calhoun 1993: 222).

While people all around the world thought with their familial arrangements – and often with some form of patriarchal concepts – this brief book focuses on English-language literature, most of it written in Western countries. Throughout the text, I have tried to balance writing in an accessible way, and using technical terms which make it possible to describe very complicated parts of changing societies with some precision, and without using too many words. I enlisted the assistance of several thoughtful neighbours from a remote farming community to help me iron out passages which still did not quite work.

Notes

1 See Claude Lévi-Strauss, *Totemism* (1962). The book's most oft-cited phrase is: 'natural species are chosen [as totems] not because they are "good to eat" but because they are "good to think"'.
2 For example, Rayna Rapp and Faye Ginsburg wrote an essay on how being parents of disabled children gave them practical experience on which they then based creative rethinking of the public sphere (Rapp and Ginsburg 2004).

References

Bacchi, Carol (2009) *Analysing Policy: What's the problem represented to be?* French's Forest, NSW: Pearson Education.

Calhoun, Craig (1993) 'Nationalism and Ethnicity', *Annual Review of Sociology* 19: 211–239.

Chakrabarty, Dipesh (2000) *Provincializing Europe: Postcolonial thought and historical difference.* Princeton, NJ: Princeton University Press.

Chakrabarty, Dipesh (2007) 'New introduction' in *Provincialising Europe: Postcolonial thought and historical difference.* Princeton, NJ: Princeton University Press.

Connell, Raewyn (2011) *Confronting Equality: Gender, knowledge and social change.* Sydney: Allen and Unwin.

Entman, Robert M. (1993) 'Framing: Toward clarification of a fractured paradigm' *Journal of Communication* 43(4): 51–58.

Kertzer, David I. and Jennie Keith (1984) *Age and Anthropological Theory.* Ithaca, NY: Cornell University Press.

Lévi-Strauss, Claude (1962) *Totemism.* London: Merlin Press.

Miller, Pavla (1998) *Transformations of Patriarchy in the West, 1500–1900.* Bloomington: Indiana University Press.

Ortner, Sherry B. (1996) *Making Gender: The politics and erotics of culture.* Boston, MA: Beacon Press.

Rapp, Rayna and Faye Ginsburg (2004) 'Enabling Disability: Renarrating kinship, reimagining citizenship', in Joan W. Scott and Debra Keates (eds) *Going Public: Feminism and the shifting boundaries of the private sphere.* Urbana: University of Illinois Press, pp. 178–200.

Stoler, Anne L. (1995) *Race and the Education of Desire: Foucault's History of Sexuality and the colonial order of things.* Durham, NC: Duke University Press.

2

REMEMBERING ROME AND READING THE BIBLE

In 1861, the British legal scholar Henry Sumner Maine published a book which soon became one of the cornerstones of what came to be called the patriarchal theory of human origins. Maine reconstructed what he believed to be the origins of humanity from Old Testament accounts of the Hebrew patriarchs in Lower Asia, and then traced the development of 'civilisation' through changes in Roman law. His Anglican churchgoing audience, he assumed, was already familiar with part of the story. As he put it:

> The chief lineaments of such [an original patriarchal] society, as collected from the early chapters in Genesis, I need not attempt to depict with any minuteness, both because they are familiar to most of us from our earliest childhood, and because, from the interest once attaching to the controversy which takes its name from the debate between Locke and Filmer, they fill a whole chapter … in English literature.

> *(Maine 1917 [1861]: Ch. 5)*

This chapter provides an overview of both sources of thinking with patriarchy. Chapter 3 deals with absolutism and democracy, issues that

Maine described as the debate between Locke and Filmer. Chapter 4 surveys nineteenth-century theorisations of human origins, and the place of patriarchy and matriarchy in what was seen as a unilineal history of humanity.

Remembering Rome

Between its foundation in the eighth century BCE and the first centuries of the Common Era, 'Rome' expanded from a small city state to a world empire covering much of the Mediterranean and Asia Minor and stretching as far as what is today France, England and Belgium in the west and Egypt, Syria and Turkey in the east. During centuries of war, conquest, colonisation and coalition making, what came to be designated as Roman law developed from many sources. The customary unwritten laws of diverse peoples, regions and cities, conventions established by merchants, armies and long-distance traders, the edicts of rulers and law-giving assemblies and the opinions of legal scholars constituted an overlapping, developing and often logically contradictory collection of precepts with which disputes could be settled and community peace and order maintained. While Greek philosophers were distinguished by their systematic reflections about the principles of justice, Roman jurists were distinctive in attempting to bring order into the messy diversity of actual legal practices. Over time, their efforts resulted in a vast corpus of written material. By the time the last influential codification of Roman law was commissioned by the emperor Justinian in the early sixth century CE, the Roman Empire as a political and territorial power was defeated in the west and began to decline in the east.

In instructing the jurist Tribonian to review all Roman laws, Justinian set out to purify, simplify and codify both scholarship and practice. The mass of legal precepts, learned treatises, commentaries, explanations and disputes had become so great, and included so many refinements and different points of view, that it seemed desirable to Justinian to eliminate that which was wrong, obscure, or repetitive, to resolve conflicts and doubts, and to organise what was worth retaining into a logically coherent and systematic form (Merryman and Pérez-Perdomo 2007: 7). In the process (which included the physical destruction of superfluous manuscripts) Roman law could be restored to its former glory. In effect, Justinian was the last of many notable Roman rulers to commission a grand – and as it turned out spectacularly successful – project of 'invented tradition'. The final product of this massive scholarly undertaking came to be called the *Corpus Iuris Civilis*. It came in three parts. The *Codex* recorded the then current law. The *Digest* or *Pandects* was a collection of key passages from the writings of Roman jurists, arranged in fifty books and subdivided into titles according to subject matter. The third part, the brief and accessible *Institutiones* (or *Institutes*) was initially conceived as an introductory textbook. The *Corpus Iuris Civilis* was rediscovered in the late eleventh century. In the centuries which followed, it had a profound influence on both secular and ecclesiastical legal development: Justinian's *Institutes* was perhaps the most widely studied textbook in Western history.

To historians familiar with debates on women's property rights, domestic violence and masters and servants' legislation in Anglo-American jurisdictions, the descriptions, explanations and logical principles outlined in the *Institutes* would feel immediately familiar. Particularly recognisable are passages explaining how the legal powers of individual Roman patriarchs were to be translated into rules for dealing with contract, property and leaseholds; the principle that a promise that cannot be converted into money does not create a legal obligation and hence is unenforceable; and the fact that patriarchs and those within their authority cannot sue each other, since dependents are incorporated into the master's legal entity (in technical terms, the legal presumption of unity of persons such as that between the *paterfamilias* and the *filius-familias*). As made clear in the *Institutes*, a key reason for articulating patriarchal rights over persons in terms of property was that *paterfamilias* was also the most common word for a property owner (so that, for example, the appropriate translation of *diligentissimus paterfamilias* is 'a most careful owner' [Krueger 1987: 114–115]) and property often consisted of slaves. The basic rule that 'owners get whatever slaves acquire' was modified to deal with situations when an owner leased a slave or other property to someone else. In this case, 'with slaves in whom you only have a usufruct, the received opinion is that whatever they get through your property or by their work accrues to you but what they obtain by other means goes to their owner'. This principle initially applied to both slaves and kin within the authority of a *paterfamilias*, but was later modified, in complicated ways, with respect to children and wives (Krueger 1987: 67). Today, throughout capitalist economies, the same basic principles still guide relations between employers and workers.

For several centuries following the collapse of the Western Roman Empire, its legal principles survived, in simplified form, as the personal law of a number of Latin peoples in medieval Europe. They also influenced some territorial systems of laws, and formed the basis of canon law, the evolving body of precepts for the governance of Christian churches and congregations. Justinian's legal compilations were rediscovered in Italy in the late eleventh century. As new universities were founded in late medieval Europe, the *Corpus Iuris Civilis* became one of the cornerstones of their curricula, and inspired parallel systematisations of canon law. Rather than deal with the body of rules enacted or customarily followed by petty sovereigns, noble landholders, local towns or merchants' guilds and their crazy patchwork of local and superior courts, universities considered canon law and the *Corpus Iuris Civilis* (both taught in Latin) as the only forms of law which possessed the universal character expected of scholarly disciplines. Until the seventeenth century, no European university offered instruction in the actual law of the land; royal directives to teach in the vernacular, and to instruct future lawyers about local rather than Roman law, tended to meet strenuous resistance from university teachers (Stein 1999: 57, 105–106). Conversely, the corpus of systematic legal erudition helped define the nature of university study and scholarly pursuits more generally.

Today, Europe and its former colonies are considered to belong to either of two legal traditions. Common law followed the dramatic expansion of the British Empire during the eighteenth and nineteenth centuries. It is today used in Great Britain, Ireland, the United States, Canada, Australia and New Zealand, and has had substantial influence on the law of many nations in Asia and Africa (Merryman and Pérez-Perdomo 2007: 3–4). Civil law is used in continental Europe, all of Latin America, many parts of Asia and Africa, and a few enclaves in the common law world. The core of the civil law tradition are formal rules enunciated by rulers or law-giving assemblies, and formulated and explained by legal scholars. Here, judges are supposed to give 'voice to the law' they themselves have no part in making. In common law countries, in contrast, judges are expected to make decisions on the basis of precedent, or previous judicial decisions dealing with comparable cases (Merryman and Pérez-Perdomo 2007: 56–57). Roman law has exerted a more direct and pervasive influence on civil law than on common law jurisdictions: it informed countless efforts to systematise legal precepts and unify multiple bodies of customary law. From the sixteenth century, in some localities and jurisdictions – among them Germany, Bohemia, Hungary, Poland and Scotland – Roman law was formally 'received' as a superior body of rules which should supersede local precepts. Elsewhere, unwritten customary law was given precedence, but attempts to make such customs uniform and logically coherent drew on the organisation, format and categories supplied by Roman law – not least because university-educated jurists staffed royal bureaucracies. As two scholars recently put it:

> It is difficult to overstate the influence of the civil law tradition on the law of specific nations, the law of international organizations, and international law... Roman ways of thinking have certainly percolated into every Western legal system. In this sense, all Western lawyers are Roman lawyers.
>
> *(Merryman and Pérez-Perdomo 2007: 3, 11)*

In the nineteenth century, a number of European states adopted civil legal codes based on Roman law. The subject matter of the most famous of these, the French *Code Napoleon* of 1804, was almost identical with the subject matter of the first three books of Justinian's legal compilation.

In England and later the wider Anglo-American common law world, the extent of Roman influence on common law was – and remains – hotly contested (Scrutton [1885] 1985). Nevertheless, even the most sceptical commentators agree that its influence was considerable. In the first place, English common law courts coexisted with several other specialised courts, such as ecclesiastical courts and equity courts, which drew extensively on Roman law (Stein 1999: 87). Second, Roman law dominated university study. Even when English universities were instructed to teach actual local legal practice and principles, or when scholars attempted to systematise common law, Roman law was used as a guide. Two famous and influential compilations of English common law, Edward Coke's *Institutes of the Laws of England* (1628–1644) and William Blackstone's *Commentaries on the Laws of England* (1765–1769) both used Justinian's *Institutes* as their model (Scrutton [1885] 1985).

As an accessible and elegant overview, the four volumes of Blackstone's *Commentaries on the Laws of England* had a disproportionate influence on eighteenth- and nineteenth-century understandings of common law and on legal practice in Anglo-American jurisdictions. Today, the work is one of the standard references in histories of married women's property legislation, as well as in accounts of the more recent history of outlawing rape in marriage. Blackstone's passages on the principles governing what he explicitly called patriarchal legal relations were particularly close to those outlined in the *Institutes*. As Blackstone saw it, their core was the conversion of mastery into two forms of property initially associated with the regulations of slave ownership. The first principle, *quicquid acquietur servo acquietur domino*, held that whatever was acquired by the servant (or wife) was acquired by the master (Krauss 1984: 515–516). The second principle, of *quod servitiium amisit* (by which the master lost the service), meant that injury to a servant, wife or child by a third party, like damage to buildings or other property, was recoverable by the master. A dependant, however, could not sue others for injury to the head of household, not least because residence in the employer's household resulted in the partial merger of the servant or other dependent into the legal persona of the master.

Debates about these principles continue into the present. In the late 1970s, for example, a series of Irish Law Reform Commission papers discussed the advisability of replacing provisions derived from Roman law with ones reflecting new forms of non-proprietorial family relations. In particular, it questioned the continued reliance on Roman law notions of master and servant in articulating a husband's ownership of his wife's and children's services, and his right to sue another for the seduction of his wife (The Law Reform Commission, Ireland 1978; 1979a; 1979b).

Blackstone's highly influential text is a good example of the complex historical status of legal compendia. Despite the work's importance as a widely used handbook for eighteenth- and nineteenth-century lawyers, justices of the peace and legislators, the *Commentaries* are not a straightforward description of actual legal practice. In England, historians note,

Blackstone made common law appear much more systematic, and links to Roman precedents more organic and seamless, than they actually were. His work can only be used as one among many sources in reconstructing the way that different groups of people in diverse localities and jurisdictions were actually governed. In addition, as legal scholars routinely remind us, laws are not the same as social relations: the most authoritative legal compendia, and even actual laws and statutes, only provide an approximation of the way contemporary disputes were settled, and a less reliable guide again to relations among and between individuals and social groups.

My argument so far, then, is not about how European men and women actually lived their lives in the past, but about a powerful discursive tradition that affected the way relations between them were thought about, debated, contested and reinvented, by both the rulers and the ruled. In particular, elements of Roman law continued to play a significant part in Western legal history centuries after the fall of Rome as a colonial power. Of course, the local content of laws varied widely, interacted in different ways with local customs, and changed over time. The fact remains that in mid-eighteenth-century England, Sir Henry Maine could assert, with great authority, that contemporary laws relating to marriage emerged from a combination of canon law and (the Roman) *ius comune*. In this sense at least, 'classical patriarchy' retained significance over two millennia of Western world history.

For the argument which follows, what is important is not only the content of actual laws but the way they were studied and taught, and legal scholarship more generally. The university study of law was considered to involve far more than mastery of local ways of adjudicating disputes. Rather, from the thirteenth to the nineteenth century, jurists and scholarly commentators argued consistently that laws constituted a privileged vantage point for understanding society as a whole. While some sought to understand laws as situated in a particular time and place, influential schools of legal scholarship treated the Roman law as 'written reason' from which, as in mathematics, could be deduced universal philosophical principles. 'Jurisprudence is the true philosophy' – a formula taken from the first sentence of Justinian's legal compendium, the *Pandects* – was among the first lessons learned by generations of law students. This powerful claim was justified in two ways. First, law constituted a true science of society (*civilis scientia*), since it was universal and viewed the world in terms of cause and effect. Second, unlike natural science, the principal object of law was the common good of society (Kelley 1978: 352–353).

Other groups of legal scholars agreed that the study of law should constitute the basis of humanist education. However, they tried to discover true principles of law from what they took to be the fundamental and universal characteristics of human nature, and based the study of law on 'juristic anthropology'. Logically, the argument went, one needed to understand the essence of something before working out how to deal with it: the art of making, interpreting and applying laws needed to be informed by understanding the 'the nature of man'. For Hegel (1770–1831), one of the leading scholars at the University of Berlin, the surviving products of classical antiquity were at once the source of profound and enduring philosophical questions, materials to think with, detailed and meaningful features of specific historical periods, and embodiments of particular stages in the progression of human thought. Hegel had a profound influence on several key protagonists in the intellectual history of patriarchy, including Marx and Engels in the nineteenth century, and the French feminist philosopher Luce Irigaray in the twentieth century.

Classical education

Important as it was, legal scholarship and practice constituted only one of the sources of Roman influence on nineteenth-century Europe. More generally, 'Rome' infused what became a transnational system of higher learning based on the Classics: the study of Latin and ancient Greek languages, and texts written by classical Greek and Roman poets, philosophers, jurists, orators and statesmen. First elaborated in Renaissance Italy, the curriculum of fifteenth- and sixteenth-century 'Latin schools' gradually came to dominate what it meant to be educated throughout the West. In eighteenth- and nineteenth-century Europe and its colonies, the Classics had become the common literary foundation of advanced learning, professional knowledge, and polite culture more generally. In communities where school attendance for more than two years of an ordinary person's life was unusual and literacy in one's mother tongue by no means universal, the mastery of Latin became a powerful marker of status. Without Latin, a man could not enter the professions, the church, or the higher ranks of government service; even if they were willing to undertake years of arduous study, care was taken to exclude lads from modest backgrounds – and most women – from too much learning. The study of Latin and Greek grammar was believed to develop the mental discipline required to regulate one's own conduct and to command others; detailed knowledge of classical works was thought to cultivate moral sense and aesthetic discernment; more prosaically, it sorted those deemed qualified to assume well-paid and influential positions in society from those who were not.

To many nineteenth-century scholars reflecting on the rapidly expanding canvas of human history, the domestic arrangements of Athenian senators and Roman nobles were more familiar than those of labouring poor in their own city. As one German contemporary put it, 'We learned about the construction of bridges built by Caesar ... but not about the construction of the German Empire... The historical and political foundations of our life remained completely unknown to us' (cited in Albisetti 1983: 3, 140, 49).

Classical learning and the formal study of law was overwhelmingly directed to men – it was men who taught Classics and boys who attended village Latin schools, town grammar schools, great public schools and universities. Yet elite and studious women – and the labouring poor – were not totally excluded from classical culture. Allusions to it were everywhere: in 'polite' conversation, literature, furnishings, politics, painting, architecture, philosophy and fashions. Alarmed by popular uses of ancient history, the French scholar Fustel de Coulanges devoted his whole life to showing that mistaken identification of his contemporaries with Greeks and Romans led to what he believed were erroneous demands for political democracy. As he put it in introduction to his most influential book, *The Ancient City* (1864):

> In our system of education, we live from infancy in the midst of the Greeks and Romans, and have become accustomed continually to compare them with ourselves, to judge of their history by our own, and to explain our revolutions by theirs. What we have received from them leads us to believe that we resemble them ... Hence spring many errors ...
>
> *(de Coulanges 1980 [1864]: 3)*

Reading the Bible and making church law

The same peoples whose legal codes were collected and systematised on Emperor Justinian's orders were described in the Bible. The Old Testament, containing the sacred scriptures of the Jewish faith, was written by a number of different authors, in several different languages, between about 1200 and 165 BCE. The New Testament books were written by Christians in the first century CE. Parts of both Testaments are also regarded as divine revelation by Muslims. The original texts include accounts and interpretations of historical events, letters to disciples, advice about living a virtuous life, prophecies, stories with everyday examples of proper conduct, passionate poetry, legal opinions, proverbs, explanations of the relationship between individuals, clergy and God, and prayers and liturgies.

In the centuries which followed the emergence of Christianity, translations and interpretations of Biblical texts were incorporated into the devotional practices of decentralised local congregations, related in different ways to Roman law, codified in different edicts of church fathers and versions of canon law, and interpreted in different ways in learned commentaries. In some periods and regions, ecclesiastical and secular administration was centralised and in others decentralised; local rules developed for resolving discrepancies between secular and church governance were contested when the balance of power shifted, or new congregations and churches formed.

By the time the first universities were founded in late medieval Europe, Christians were governed by a tangle of overlapping, inconsistent and often contradictory precepts, which related in different ways to secular rule. Around 1140, in order to bring order into chaos and make canon law a suitable object of university study, a scholarly Benedictine monk from Bologna set out to systematise it. As the jurist Tribonian did before him, Gratian consulted existing compilations of laws and decrees, the recoded pronouncements of prominent church leaders, and the commentaries written by respected scholars. Inspired by the *Corpus Iuris Civilis*, Gratian's *Concordantia Discordantium Canonum* (or Harmony of Contradictory Laws) went a long way to resolving contradictory precepts and conflicting texts and producing a systematic treatise suitable for university study. The *Decretum Gratiani* dealt with issues such as sources of canon law, ordinations, religious communities, ecclesiastical property, the buying and selling of absolution from sin, those who disregarded the teachings and authority of the church, marriage, penance, and sacraments. First used at the University of Bologna, the *Decretum* soon became the basis of education in canon law in other early European universities, such as those in Paris, Orléans, Canterbury, Oxford and Padua.

In the centuries which followed, the *Decretum* continued to be used in the teaching of canon law and church administration. It was annotated and commented on by the most illustrious scholars; it provided a foundation for papal decisions on contested points of canon law, as well as a basis for further systematic compilations. The *Decretum Gratiani* became the first part of the *Corpus Juris Canonici*, the great body of canon law published in 1500, and served as an important source for the official codification of Catholic canon law in 1917 and its revision in 1983.

During the Reformation of the sixteenth century, a number of congregations rejected the political and spiritual leadership of the Roman Catholic Church and formed new Protestant churches, with their own interpretations of Biblical texts, appropriate devotional practices, and relations between ecclesiastical and secular authority (or church and state). While rejecting important aspects of canon law, new churches drew on it extensively in working out their own rules and regulations. The Church of England developed its own version of canon law, and this was generally accepted in the churches of the Anglican Communion. In turn, the institutions and concepts of canon law continued to interact with the Roman-based secular law and jurisprudence in both Catholic and Protestant regions. They affected marriage law, the law of obligations, the doctrine of modes of property acquisition, possession, wills, legal persons, the law of criminal procedure, and the law concerning proof or evidence.[1]

Debates about the Bible and proper conduct of Christian denominations were not confined to theologians, princes and priests. Throughout Europe and its colonies, generations of lay people debated the respective places of the Old and New Testaments, interpretations of Biblical passages dealing with relations between women and men, parents and children, church hierarchy and laity, God and individual worshippers, masters and servants, lords and commoners. Church fathers cited the words of God to defend their own and worldly authority. Visionaries, rebellious peasants, communities of nuns reluctant to accept the authority of priests, and pious Christians disgusted by greedy and dissolute masters and corrupt church officials, countered with contrasting Biblical passages to argue for change. In articulating grievances, defending or pursuing their interests or setting up new Christian communities, contemporaries tended to think with patriarchy as outlined in the Bible, since that was the language in which the relations of authority were routinely articulated (Visser 't Hooft 1982). Many heresies included well-argued claims that women played a prominent role in the early Christian church, and that they were entitled – through tradition, faith and wisdom – to preach and hold leadership positions in their congregations (Gaden 1981). 'Nowadays everyone thinks he is a master of the Scripture', Luther complained in the 1520s, 'and every Tom, Dick and Harry imagines he understand the Bible and knows it inside out'. This was quite wrong, he went on:

> all the other arts and skills have their preceptors and masters from whom one must learn, and they have rules and laws to be obeyed and adhered to. Only Holy Scripture and the Word of God seems to be open to everybody's vanity, pride, whim and arrogance, and is twisted and warped according to everybody's own head. That is why we have so much trouble now with factions and sects.
>
> *(Quoted in Strauss 1984: 113)*[2]

Some Christian denominations, proclaiming the priesthood of all believers, decided to place a vernacular translation of the Bible into the hands of every parishioner. Others, more cautious, preferred to keep the Scriptures in the hands of specialists, and conduct most of church business in Latin. Neither approach guaranteed that Christians were familiar with approved interpretations of the Bible. When authorities bothered to make systematic enquiries, as they did in both Catholic and Protestant regions of seventeenth century Europe, they found that a large proportion of parishioners could not give satisfactory answers about the most basic principles of their faith; those best informed were at times also the most rebellious. Even worse, people tenaciously clung to their old beliefs. They said the Lord's Prayer while casting lead to tell fortunes. They gathered occult substances on Christian holidays and invoked the names of the Father, the Son, and the Holy Ghost to protect chickens from hawks and humans from the evil eye. They rang church bells against storms and hail, addressed Christian prayers to the devil, and used altar vessels to locate missing objects. Village healers cured cattle of worms by spitting three times in appeal to the Trinity. Wise women called on God to bless the crystal in which they saw the face of a thief. Worse still, they concocted infusions of baptismal water against bed-wetting and chanted gospel verses while curing or inflicting injury (Strauss 1978: 262, 303–304; 1988: 195).

* * *

Debates about interpretations and implications of Biblical patriarchy are not a thing of the past. Today they continue to inform keenly contested secular and church laws such as those regarding property relations, the place of women in Christian congregations, marriage, sexuality, abortion, relations between spouses, and sexual abuse of women and children. The Bible, a prominent twentieth-century theologian noted, contains not only patriarchal tradition but also a prophetic critique of that tradition (Visser 't Hooft 1982: 54). More broadly, as Ann Braude, director of the Women's Studies in Religion programme at Harvard University, put it in her address on the occasion of the 50th anniversary of the admission of women to its Divinity School:

> Religion's role in constructing, maintaining, distorting, and subverting gender is played out every day in headlines and in homes and schools throughout the world; in debates over birth control, abortion, and family violence that spill into both domestic and foreign policy; in debates about the Iraqi constitution and the American invasion of Afghanistan; about the nature of marriage; about health, law, development, and globalization.
>
> *(Braude 2006: 379–380)*

Liberation theology, with roots in Latin America, for example, is built around the claim that defending the rights of the poor is the central aspect of the gospel. It follows that true followers of Jesus must align themselves with those who have historically been marginalised or deprived of their rights, address the suffering and oppression of the poor, work towards a just society, and bring about social and political change.[3] The place of women in Christian churches is another current debate conducted in terms of Biblical passages. The patriarchal image of God and the masculinity of Jesus and his disciples have for centuries been used to exclude women from full participation in the life of the church, defend the male-dominated church hierarchy, and enforce women's sacramental dependence on men. In contrast, Quaker 'ministry' – the right to speak during a Quaker meeting – was open to women from the beginnings of the movement in the 1650s. A number of churches now allow the ordination of women; others, such as the Catholic Church, remain implacably opposed to it.[4]

Leadership roles in the church involve not just an expansion of the pool of eligible candidates, but the rethinking of fundamental dimensions of doctrine and faith. A number of feminist theologians and pro-feminist men dispute whether Christ's disciples correctly interpreted his words and the events in his life; others argue that the customs of peoples several thousand years ago do not provide appropriate guidance for contemporary social relations. Yet others question the depiction of God as male and a father, and argue that the maleness of Jesus is irrelevant in theological tradition (Schneiders 1986; Braude 2004). Some scholars have gone on to rethink the whole corpus of Christian texts, doctrines, practices and history in order to reveal and remedy their bias against women (see for example Daly 1968; Coakley 2013).

The personal characteristics of the faithful have also come under scrutiny, with a number of pro-feminist men contributing to attempts to come up with non-patriarchal forms of inclusive church leadership and masculine spirituality (see for example Visser 't Hooft 1982; Gelfer 2009). In contrast, anti-feminist men (and some women) have attempted to reinvent biblical patriarchy so it would appeal to a broad conservative audience, and composed passionate calls on men to reclaim patriarchal powers and duties as described in the Bible. As the author of a website named Righteous Warriors put it:

> Biblical Patriarchy is the essence and timeless aspect of the Hebraic Roots … A patriarch is a family ruler. He is the man in charge.

Biblical Patriarchy is a social system in which the father is the head of the family, and men have authority over their women and children. Satan has done a masterful job of seducing our society. Men are no longer real men. Women who Elohim [God] made to be the helpmeet of man have become the rulers of man. Most men today don't hold a candle compared to the brilliant light that shines through the men of the Old Testament … They were men of destiny who understood or who came to understand their place and calling in Elohim. They fought the enemy and overcame. They refused to submit to the tyranny of government when it opposed Elohim and they were willing to die rather than to be found compromising Scriptures.

Notes

1 www.britannica.com/topic/canon-law, accessed 19 October 2016.
2 Although Luther originally translated the Bible into vernacular German, he now believed that it should be read by the small minority versed in Greek, Latin or Hebrew so it could be understood 'properly'.
3 www.gotquestions.org/liberation-theology.html. In the 1980s, the movement was condemned by the Catholic Church's Sacred Congregation for the Doctrine of the Faith for its use of ideas taken from Karl Marx (Wiesner-Hanks 2015: 350).
4 For example, some national Presbyterian churches began ordaining women in the late nineteenth century, others more recently, yet others continue to ordain men only or reversed their earlier decision to ordain women. Since the 1980s, some Anglican and Protestant churches have appointed women as bishops.

References

Albisetti, James C. (1983) *Secondary School Reform in Imperial Germany*. Princeton, NJ: Princeton University Press.

Braude, Ann (2004) *Transforming the Faiths of Our Fathers: The women who changed American religion*. Basingstoke: Palgrave Macmillan.

Braude, Ann (2006) 'A Short Half-century: Fifty years of women at Harvard Divinity School', *Harvard Theological Review* 99(4): 369–380.

Coakley, Sarah (2013) *God, Sexuality and the Self: An essay 'On the Trinity'*. Cambridge: Cambridge University Press.

Daly, Mary (1968) *The Church and the Second Sex*. New York: Harper & Row.

de Coulanges, Fustel (1980 [1864]) *The Ancient City: A study of the religion, laws, and institutions of Greece and Rome*. Baltimore, MD: Johns Hopkins University Press.

Gaden, John R. (1981) 'Reclaiming their Freedom: Women and the church', Ch. 2 in Norma Grieve and Pat Grimshaw (eds) *Australian Women: Feminist perspectives*. Melbourne: Oxford University Press, pp. 15–24.

Gelfer, Joseph (2009) *Numen, Old Men: Contemporary masculine spiritualities and the problem of patriarchy*. London: Equinox Publishing.

Kelley, Donald R. (1978) 'The Metaphysics of Law: An essay on the very young Marx', *The American Historical Review* 83(2): 250–267.

Krauss, E. P. (1984) 'On the Distinction between Real and Personal Property', *Seton Hall Law Review* 14: 485–519.

Krueger, Paul (1987) *Justinian's Institutes*. Translated with an introduction by Peter Birks and Grant McLeod. Ithaca, NY: Cornell University Press.

Maine, Sir Henry (1917 [1861]) 'Primitive Society and Ancient Law', Ch. 5 of *Ancient Law*. London: Dent.

Merryman, John Henry and Rogelio Pérez-Perdomo (2007) *The Civil Law Tradition: An introduction to the legal systems of Europe and Latin America*. 3rd edn. Stanford, CA: Stanford University Press.

Righteous Warriors (n.d.) https://www.righteouswarriors.com/controversial/article3.html, accessed 17 October 2016.

Schneiders, Sandra Marie (1986) 'Women and the Word: The gender of God in the New Testament and the spirituality of women'. Madeleva Lecture in spirituality. Costa Mesa, CA: Paulist Press.

Scrutton, Thomas Edward ([1885] 1985) *The Influence of the Roman Law on the Law of England*. Cambridge: Cambridge University Press. Reprint, Littleton, CO: Rothman & Co.

Stein, Peter (1999) *Roman Law in European History*. Cambridge: Cambridge University Press.

Strauss, Gerald (1978) *Luther's House of Learning: Indoctrination of the young in the German Reformation*. Baltimore, MD: Johns Hopkins University Press.

Strauss, Gerald (1984) 'Lutheranism and Literacy: A reassessment', in Kaspar von Greyerz (ed.) *Religion and Society in Early Modern Europe*. London: George Allen and Unwin.

Strauss, Gerald (1988) 'The Social Function of Schools in the Lutheran Reformation in Germany', *History of Education Quarterly* 28(2): 191–206.

The Law Reform Commission, Ireland (1978) 'The Law Relating to Criminal Conversation and the Enticement and Harbouring of a Spouse', Working paper no. 5.

The Law Reform Commission, Ireland (1979a) 'The Law Relating to Seduction and the Enticement and Harbouring of a Child', Working paper no. 6.

The Law Reform Commission, Ireland (1979b) 'The Law Relating to Loss of Consortium and Loss of Services of a Child', Working paper no. 7.

Visser 't Hooft, Willem (1982) *The Fatherhood of God in an Age of Emancipation*. Geneva: World Council of Churches.

Wiesner-Hanks, Merry E. (2015) *A Concise History of the World*. Cambridge: Cambridge University Press.

3

ABSOLUTISM, DEMOCRACY AND GOD

In the last forty years, many feminist commentators claimed that state power is patriarchal. Others disputed such claims; yet others argued that governments should be more rather than less fatherly. Such disputes have a long pedigree. The explicitly patriarchal character of territorial and ecclesiastical rule had been contested for centuries – by disaffected communities of believers, towns with a proud heritage of municipal governance, social groups convinced that they should have a say in decisions affecting their lives. One such dispute occurred 400 years ago, in an era when modern states began to emerge in Europe. On one side were those who argued that a God-ordained patriarchal family was the ideal model of absolutist power, on the other those for whom a social contract between free citizens was a more appropriate model of rule. Inspired and taken up by powerful social groups, the dispute had far-reaching historical consequences. In its regional variations, it also became part of standard accounts of the development of modern democracies.

Absolutism and monarchs' God-given patriarchal power

In 1576, in a country ravaged by religious wars, the French philosopher and jurist Jean Bodin outlined his conviction that peace could be restored if the monarch was accorded absolute and indivisible power. The well-ordered family, he explained, is a true image of the commonwealth, and domestic comparable with sovereign authority. Just as in Christian lands one God ruled the universe, so territorial states should be governed by single fatherly rulers. Like God, the king was the head of the body and the shepherd of the flock. And just as God does not ask the advice or seek the consent of lower orders of creation, so genuine monarchs should not seek the consent of their subjects. However, monarchs should obey God and the law of nature. Since these protected private property, a monarch should obtain his subject's consent before imposing new taxes. And because the rule of women was against divine, natural, and human law, no woman should ever become a monarch (Hill 1964: 459; Vincent 1987: 47; 'Jean Bodin (c. 1529–1596)')

In England, the patriarchal theory of obligation constituted the official doctrine of the Anglican Church and was accepted by the dissenting clergy. During the reign of James I (who too called himself *parens patriae*), it was further elaborated and linked to absolutist political theory. 'In a family, the master or *paterfamilias*, who is a kind of petty monarch there, hath authority to prescribe to his children and servants', a seventeenth-century sermon by Robert Sanderson pointed out. It followed that:

> what power the master hath over his servants for the ordering of his family, no doubt the same at least, if not much more, hath the supreme magistrate over his subjects, for the peaceable ordering of the commonwealth: the magistrate being *pater patriae* as the master is *paterfamilias*.
>
> *(Quoted in Hill 1964: 461)*

Perhaps the most famous exposition of what came to be called patriarchalism was written on the eve of its demise in the mid-seventeenth century by the English country gentleman and scholar Robert Filmer in his *Patriarcha*, or *The Natural Power of Kings*. Drawing heavily on Bodin, Filmer argued that political hierarchy, obedience and authority were natural; just as children were born naturally subject to their father, all people were naturally subject to their king. And because monarchs' authority was originally inherited from Adam, it was divinely ordained (Schochet 1969: 434–435; see also Steinfeld 1991: 57–59).

Throughout early modern Europe, Lutheran and Calvinist princes, Catholic monarchs and Protestant kings all called themselves father to their people (Po-Chia Hsia 1989: 148; see also Hill 1964: 459).[1] Paternal authority was invoked by princes, magistrates, pastors and schoolmasters to justify their power. Contemporary catechisms, whether in Stuart England or Lutheran Germany, reiterated the same principles. The Commandment regarding children's obedience to their parents was invariably interpreted to cover also what were considered to be essentially identical relations of servants and apprentices to their masters, and subjects to their magistrates, priests, lords and kings. According to Luther's *Larger Catechism* of 1529:

> All other forms of authority flow from and are extension of parental authority ... Thus all those who are called 'lords' stand in the parent's stead and necessarily take their power and authority from [the parental office]. Therefore the Bible calls them all 'fathers', because they exercise in their rule the office of a father and ought to regard their folk with a fatherly heart.
>
> *(Quoted in Brady 1986: 36)*

A 1689 English catechism spelt out the link between parental and political authority even more explicitly:

> These words, Father and Mother, include all superiours, as well as a Civil Parent (the king and his Magistrates, a Master, a Mistress, or an Husband) and an Ecclesiastical Parent (the Bishop and Ministers) as the natural parent that begat and bore thee: To all these I owe Reverance and Obediance, Service and Maintenance, Love and Honour.
>
> *(Quoted in Schochet 1969: 433)*

It followed that democracy would be 'a manifest breach of the Fifth Commandment' (quoted in Hill 1964: 459).

Patriarchalism and democracy

Compelling as it was, the parallel between domestic, political and Godly authority did not provide sufficient guidance for the administration of increasingly complex territorial units. Neither did it convince increasingly powerful social groups opposing absolutist powers. The patriarchal household, the critics argued, was not an appropriate model of political governance. In seventeenth-century England, Germany and France, social contract theorists such as the Englishman John Locke (1632–1704) and the Frenchman Jean-Jacques Rousseau (1712–1778) rejected most – though not all – of the axioms of patriarchalist political theory. Their arguments typically started by claiming that the family itself is not, should not or need not be characterised by the despotic and absolute rule of the father and husband, and therefore does not provide a clear model of natural and lifelong patriarchal subordination for the rest of society. In their support, enlightened educational writers typically argued that 'parental tyranny' has dire social consequences. To prevent strife and disappointment, children should be brought up firmly but lovingly and without violence to internalise the appropriate moral virtues. Children must be made obedient, and parents establish, as soon as possible, entire and absolute authority over them. But this should be done through affection, reason, benevolence and understanding rather than force, love rather than fear and violence, guided freedom rather than constraint, in behaviour as in dress.

Similarly, the authority of husbands and the subordination of wives should be based on love and respect rather than force. More importantly, familial and political rule were distinct and do not and should not obey the same principles, not least because the family stood outside of politics. Political authority and obligation, they concluded, were conventional rather than natural; and political subjects were civil equals. Whatever was thought appropriate for daughters and wives, sons were born free and equal and, as adults, were free as their fathers before them. Government was possible and necessary as a result of a social contract entered into by these men. What they lost in giving up their natural liberty, Rousseau added in his *Social Contract* (1762), they more than compensated for by gaining in civil and moral liberty.

Like Locke, Rousseau stressed that self-mastery alone allows one an independence of all other masters and enables one eventually to live within society yet uncorrupted by the servile dependencies it encourages. Rousseau, however, rejected Locke's claim that the best way to educate children was to reason with them, and instead argued for a 'natural education', skilfully guided by a tutor's hidden hand (Fliegelman 1982: 30). Self-mastery, however, had completely different connotations for men and for women. 'When a man renounces liberty he renounces his essential manhood, his rights, and even his duty as a human being', Rousseau (1966 [1762]: 248) wrote in *The Social Contract*. Yet women, according to Book 5 of *Emile*, 'must be trained to bear the yoke from the first so that they may not feel it: to master their own caprices and submit themselves to the will of others'.

Generations of radical critics, increasingly joined by feminist commentators, have drawn attention to the fact that even in theory the eventual demise of patriarchalism as the organising principle of political life did not mean that all children would grow up to be equal under the law. The relationship between sons and fathers might have become more democratic, but servants remained subordinate to masters and women to men.

Thus seventeenth-century English Levellers saw the suffrage as the birthright of all English men (not women), but considered that servants (including wage labourers) and beggars, through their dependence on others, had forfeited their birthright to a voice in elections (Macpherson 1962: 124). Politically, servants, apprentices, women and children were simply 'included in their masters' (Hill 1964: 478). Locke insisted on the contractual nature and limitations of the relation between master and servant, yet assumed that while in his employ, the servant would be placed 'into the Family of his Master and under the ordinary Discipline thereof' (Locke (1966 [1690]: 69–70).[2] Indeed, Locke assumed that while the labouring class was a necessary part of the nation, its members were not in fact full members of the body politic and had no claims to be so, not least because, not having property, they could not live a fully rational life (Macpherson 1962: 221–222). In turn, the man who had not shown the ability to accumulate property was not a full man, and could therefore hardly be expected to govern his family.

More recent feminist reading of the texts shows that the fathers of liberal democratic theory invariably ended up agreeing with their patriarchalist opponents that women, as future wives, were – and should remain – naturally subject to men and husbands (see for example Pateman 1988; Shanley and Pateman 1991; Pateman 1988). As the political theorist Carole Pateman summarised it (1988: Ch. 5), what in fact took place was a contest between champions of two different forms of patriarchy: in the realm of political theory at least, a contract between free and equal brothers replaced the 'law of the father' with public rules which bind all men equally as brothers. Women remain subject to men, but under a different set of rules.

Notes

1 Modern dictators such as Stalin did so too: 'The state is a family, and I am your father', he often declared.
2 The same principles were expressed in Blackstone's famous eighteenth-century *Commentaries*, which grouped the duties and obligations between master and servant with those between husband and wife, parent and child, and guardian and ward, to make up what he referred to as 'the private economical relations of persons'.

References

Brady, T. A. (1986) 'Luther and the State: The reformer's teaching in its social setting', in J. D. Tracy (ed.) *Luther and the Modern State in Germany*. Ann Arbor, MI: Edwards Brothers.

Fliegelman, Jay (1982) *Prodigals and Pilgrims: The American revolution against patriarchal authority, 1750–1800*. Cambridge: Cambridge University Press.

Hill, Christopher (1964) *Society and Puritanism in Pre-revolutionary England*. London: Secker and Warburg.

Lindfors, Tommi 'Jean Bodin (c. 1529–1596)', in *The Internet Encyclopedia of Philosophy*. ISSN 2161–0002. www.iep.utm.edu/bodin/, accessed 6 December 2016.

Locke, John (1966 [1690]) 'Second Treatise on Civil Government: An essay concerning the true original, extent and end of civil government', in E. Barker (ed.) *Social Contract: Essays by Locke, Hume and Rousseau*. London: Oxford University Press.

Macpherson, C. B. (1962) *The Political Theory of Possessive Individualism: Hobbes to Locke*. London: Oxford University Press.

Pateman, Carole (1988) 'The Fraternal Social Contract: Some observations on patriarchal civil society', in John Keane (ed.) *Civil Society and the State: New European perspectives*. London: Verso.

Pateman, Carole (1988) *The Sexual Contract*. Cambridge: Polity Press.

Po-Chia Hsia, Ronnie (1989) *Social Discipline in the Reformation: Central Europe 1550–1750*. London: Routledge.

Rousseau, Jean-Jacques (1966 [1762]) 'The Social Contract', in E. Barker (ed.) *Social Contract: Essays by Locke, Hume and Rousseau*. London: Oxford University Press.

Schochet, G. J. (1969) 'Patriarchalism, Politics and Mass Attitudes in Stuart England', *The Historical Journal* 12(3): 434–435.

Shanley, Mary L. and Carole Pateman (eds) (1991) *Feminist Interpretations and Political Theory*. Philadelphia: Pennsylvania State University Press.

Steinfeld, Robert J. (1991) *The Invention of Free Labor: Employment relations in English and American law and culture, 1350–1870*. Chapel Hill: University of North Carolina Press.

Vincent, Andrew (1987) *Theories of the State*. Oxford: Blackwell.

4

PATRIARCHY, MATRIARCHY AND THE ORIGINS OF HUMANITY

Legal anthropology and revolutions in time

For centuries, people in Christian lands believed that humans and the world around them were the result of divine creation around 6,000 years ago, as calculated by biblical scholars who added up events in the Old and New Testaments.[1] By the beginning of the nineteenth century, new approaches to dating fossils, more systematic excavations, re-examination of existing collections and new discoveries enabled researchers to build up a case for overturning the Biblical chronology. The first step of this 'revolution in ethnological time', in the 1830s, hinged on the proposition that fossilised remains of plants and animals could be used to prove the immense antiquity of the Earth. For three decades, this realisation coexisted with the belief that humans were the results of the final act of creation, and that the Bible contained an accurate chronology of the totality of *human* history.

The second stage of the revolution in time was ignited by evidence that humans too predated written records by immense stretches of time, and perhaps even, as Darwin argued, evolved from non-human ancestors. Suddenly, the known world had shrunk to a small island in a vast ocean of uncharted time. During the same period, merchants, missionaries, colonial officials, sailors and explorers built up a mass of increasingly systematic information about exotic plants and animals and 'savage and primitive' peoples. In the mid-nineteenth century, a few researchers began pioneering what initially appeared as a scandalous and sacrilegious proposition: that all peoples evolved over a very long time from common primitive ancestors, and without divine intervention.[2]

Within twenty years, a number of scholars compiled new intellectual maps of the vast new terrain, and laid the foundations of the study of prehistory. Darwin's *Origin of Species* (1859) was perhaps the most influential account of evolutionary theory, positing that humans, animals and plants shared the same basic mechanism of change over time. Most of the founding classics of anthropology as a scientific discipline did not directly engage with Darwin's work, but appeared within a few years of its publication.

In charting the new terrain opened in front of them, the early anthropologists, most of them lawyers by training, reached for the familiar concepts and intellectual tools furnished by their education. These included patriarchy as described in the Bible and in Justinian's *Institutes*, more or less extensive knowledge of the Classics, scholarly techniques for reconstructing original manuscripts and law codes from carelessly copied, translated, altered and corrupted later versions, and comparative philology, with its techniques for reconstructing ancient languages from later variants. Explicitly or implicitly, most also drew on one or both classical precursors of modern anthropology. The first grew out of philosophical speculation about human nature such as that of the ancient Greek Sophists. The second approach anthropology built on were the ethnographic observations of ancient Greek and Roman historians, and was frequently associated with what came to be called 'comparative theory'. This theory, which provided one of the logical underpinnings of most nineteenth-century anthropological works, held that humans evolved along a single path leading from savagery to barbarism to civilisation. However, some cultures moved faster than others towards the marvels of nineteenth-century science, arts and industry. While no surviving human societies were stuck at the earliest stages of human development, remaining primitive tribes approximated what life was like for civilised peoples thousands of years ago: studying them was like taking a trip into the infancy of civilisation. As the famous German poet, playwright and scholar Friedrich von Schiller put it in 1789:

The discoveries which our European seafarers have made in distant oceans and on remote shores afford us a spectacle which is as instructive as it is entertaining. They show us societies arrayed around us at various levels of development, as an adult might be surrounded by children of different ages, reminded by their example of what he once was and whence he started ... But how embarrassing and dismal is the picture of our own childhood presented in these peoples ... Many have been found to be unacquainted with the most elementary skills: without iron, without the plow, some even without fire ... Here there is not even the simplest marriage tie; there no knowledge of property; here the indolent mind cannot learn even from experience that is repeated daily; savages have been seen to abandon carelessly their sleeping-places, because it did not occur to them that tomorrow they would sleep again ... Others ... have reached a higher level of civilization, but their slavery and despotism still present a horrible picture ... even where men have advanced from hostile solitude to social organization, from poverty to comfort, from fearfulness to enjoyment, how strange and barbarous they appear to us! ... Thus we were too. Caesar and Tacitus found us not much better eighteen hundred years ago.

(von Schiller 1972 [1789]: 325–326)

Some scholars expanded the theory of unilineal human evolution to argue that individual biological and even psychic development recapitulated that of the species.

Sir Henry James Sumner Maine (1822–1888)

Henry Maine was born in 1822 and was brought up in modest circumstances by his mother. Maine excelled in mathematics, Greek and Latin, graduated when he was 22, and the following year obtained his first academic job. One of the tasks he set his first students was to translate Justinian's *Institutes* from Latin into English. At the age of thirty, he accepted appointment as the first Reader in Jurisprudence and Civil Law at the Inns of Court in London. This position provided Maine with the impetus to systematise and innovate. His Inns of Court lectures became the basis of his best-known work, *Ancient Law*.

Maine was at once a conservative, a political elitist and a committed reformer. Today, he is regarded as a leading Victorian intellectual and anti-democrat, and is routinely credited with grafting anthropology onto the study of comparative law. In his own time, Maine was seen as one of the most influential proponents of the patriarchal theory of human origins: for several decades, the enormous prestige of his theory profoundly influenced the teaching of jurisprudence in Britain.

Written in 1861, Maine's *Ancient Law* was aimed at a popular audience as well as legal scholars. It was infused by Maine's profound admiration of the Classics, his legal training, and conviction that Aryan societies such as his own were dynamic while those of non-Western peoples such as those in India and China were static. Most legal texts, Maine noted, drew consciously or unconsciously on the Romans and began with speculative passages on an original state of nature. In contrast to such speculation, Maine (still assuming that human history could be reckoned in thousands rather than hundreds of thousands of years) set out to accomplish a scientific reconstruction of the earliest human organisation. Of the possible range of sources for this task, Maine identified three: the rare preserved observations of primitive peoples by their ancient civilised contemporaries, early historical records and, above all, ancient laws. Ancient laws, in turn, could be reconstructed from later versions, and deduced from a number of related though not immediately obvious laws, institutions and practices. Among these were the severe legal disabilities of married women (such as Maine's own mother) under contemporary English common law.

Just as linguists, using techniques of comparative philology, managed to reconstruct an archaic Indo-European language, Maine argued, legal scholars could apply methods of comparative jurisprudence to surviving codes of law to separate out later corruptions and amendments and to arrive at authentic archaic versions. Assuming the short chronology of human origins, Maine believed that Old Testament accounts of the Hebrew patriarchs in Lower Asia provided the requisite firm point. Unlike modern societies, Maine argued, primitive communities were not composed of individuals but rather of families as basic units; there was no individual but only collective property controlled by the patriarch. Strangers were commonly incorporated into such families through a variety of means, even as the legal fiction of common descent was maintained. The basic characteristics of Maine's primeval patriarchal order corresponded to the powers routinely attributed to the ancient Roman *paterfamilias*. The severity of the patriarch's original powers was counteracted by his obligation to provide for all those he commanded.

Maine concluded that this family form, as held together by the *patria potestas*, was 'the nidus out of which the entire Law of Persons has germinated' (Maine 1917 [1861]: 89); more generally, it was 'the germs out of which has assuredly been unfolded every form of moral restraint which controls our actions and shapes our conduct at the present moment' (Maine 1917 [1861]: 71). Despite the enormous significance of this initial social order, and the fact that systems of law remained indelibly marked by the original precepts, Maine noted that it was remarkable how quickly and comprehensively the full extent of patriarchal powers was modified in more civilised times. To trace the world historical development of this primeval patriarchal family would have been extremely difficult except for one crucial factor. Almost everywhere except Europe, Maine argued, societies failed to show the least desire to change, and so were stuck in the initial stage of compiling legal codes; only Western progressive societies kept changing and improving, and so were the only ones with genuine histories.

Having disposed of most of the world, Maine went on to describe, briefly but with considerable sophistication, the way that core aspects of patriarchal powers were transformed in Western Europe, and England in particular, with regard to sons, daughters and wives. He then traced the uneven transformations of male control over women. This happened as precepts of newly dominant Christianity, canon law with its archaic disabilities relating to wives, and the stringently patriarchal customs of less civilised peoples who defeated the Roman Empire, replaced the lax notions which had developed in latter-day Rome. The end result of these complex developments was to leave single women relatively free, as under the late Roman system, but married women subject to much earlier forms of barbaric tutelage – except now by their husbands rather than kin. This was fair enough, Maine noted, with regard to wives' personal disabilities, but outrageously injurious with regard to property. Indeed, common law relating to married women retained in it a fossilised version of the ancient barbaric patriarchal law relating to everyone. To drive the point home, Maine remarked on the various ploys with which diverse societies masked the initial similarity of slavery to aspects of ancient Roman law regarding the family.

Maine concluded the core chapter of *Ancient Law* with what has probably proved his best-known contribution to scholarship. In general, he noted, legal relations between individuals were derived from, and to some extent were still coloured by, the powers and privileges anciently residing in the patriarchal family. If such relations are designated as 'status', 'the movement of the progressive societies has hitherto been a movement from status to contract'.

Johann Jakob Bachofen (1815–1887)

Maine's contemporary, the wealthy judge and legal scholar Johann Jakob Bachofen, drew on the same intellectual heritage to propose an alternative account of human prehistory. Rather than patriarchy, his account of civilisation (after an initial period of indiscriminate sexuality) began with matriarchy. Rather than legal codes, Bachofen believed that it was myths which provided the most appropriate source materials for reconstructing the 'childhood of humanity'. Bachofen's scholarly work combined a painstakingly systematic approach with fervent emotional engagement with relics of classical culture. He also relied extensively on religious sources. The power of religion, Bachofen believed, made it possible for women to exert great influence on whole historical epochs through their 'inclination toward the supernatural and divine, the irrational and the miraculous' (Bachofen 1992: 85).

Bachofen is best known for his book *Mother Right: An Investigation of the Religious and Juridical Character of Matriarchy in the Ancient World* (1861). While Maine implicitly endorsed the shorter chronology of human development, *Mother Right* mapped out a far longer prehistory, divided into three broad periods. The first, characterised by indiscriminate sexual intercourse, was associated with the Earth. During this era, people relied on hunting, property was held in common, marriage was seen as an infringement of religious commandments, and children had communal parents. The second period, characterised by a chaste, monogamous, peaceable and generous matriarchal and matrilineal culture, was associated with settled agriculture and the Moon. At this stage of history, woman was 'the repository of all culture, of all benevolence, of all devotion, of all concern for the living and grief for the dead'. The third, patriarchal stage of humanity, characterised by private property, division of labour, and jealously guarded fathers' conjugal rights, was associated with the Sun. Violent and warlike, it alone transcended natural forces and excelled in abstract reasoning. At the core of the profound difference between a matriarchal and patriarchal order were the unavoidable facts of procreation. While maternity is for all to see, paternity can only be established and understood by the force of abstract thought. It was ancient Rome which gave paternity its strict juridical form, and so preserved it for posterity against the decadence of religion, the corruption of manners, and a popular return to matriarchal views.

Bachofen explained the passage from one phase of human history to the next through a process in which the excesses and injustices of one order led the injured sex to seek a better life through a period of violent upheaval. So women initially rebelled against the barbarism and inconvenience of unregulated sexual intercourse and established dominance based on loving models of motherly love. Then matriarchy was corrupted by carnal desires, sensual frenzy and Amazonian excesses, swamps gained preponderance over agriculture, and men vanquished warlike women. The excesses of the stern patriarchy of classical Greece and Rome which followed were themselves alleviated through women's gentle and spiritual influence, and so led to the refinements and triumphs of Western civilisation. In Africa and Asia, debased matriarchal principles continued to dominate, with wilful deification of the bestial side of human nature.

Unlike most of his colleagues, Bachofen was uninterested in people's material circumstances, changes in technology, or military conquests. Rather, his work focussed on ancient mythology, symbolism and language. Myths, he argued, preserved the collective memory. Even though they predominantly described events which did not actually happen, they unquestionably charted things which were generally thought. Indeed, the underlying ideas and storylines of myths constituted law-like and systematic manifestations of primordial thinking.

Later in life, Bachofen concluded that myths and symbols constituted a powerful and continuous, but non-rational force in human history and, beyond that, a universal law of human history. *The Myth of Tanaquil* (1870) revolves around the inward force of spiritual principles of mother and father right as shaping the destinies of historic civilisations, and underpinning profound contrasts between the Orient and the Occident. One low and basely sensuous, the other high and spiritually pure, they both originated in the same primordial stages of human development. Bachofen concluded that the myth of the woman who confers supreme power on men originated in the lustful, promiscuous and powerful figure of the Oriental female ruler. But while the West continued to develop its Roman patriarchal heritage, the Orient was stuck at a debased version of a matriarchal past.

In the late nineteenth and early twentieth centuries, Bachofen's work inspired groups of radical intellectuals focussing on revolt against father figures. With the resurgence of women's movements in the 1970s, Bachofen's work – and the idea of matriarchy more generally – inspired forms of feminist spirituality, ecofeminism, peace activism, alternative lifestyles and woman-centred collectives. African theorists of Negritude – a proud and noble heritage of the African diaspora – employed Bachofen's schema to a different purpose. Cheikh Anta Diop, for example, argued that in precolonial Africa there was no transition from matriarchy to patriarchy, since the social structure was essentially matriarchal in the sense of female rule, female transmission of property and descent, and man being the mobile element in marriage or sexual union. Fundamental changes in the African social structure began with Arabo-Islamic invasions, and became more far-reaching under European imperialism (Diop 1959). Bachofen's work remains in print today, and is among the key texts employed in a revival of 'matriarchal studies'.

John Ferguson McLennan (1827–1881)

John Ferguson McLennan was born in Scotland in 1827, one of three sons of an insurance agent. At the age of 22 he graduated in law from King's College in Aberdeen. In 1857, he was called to the Scottish bar. McLennan's habit of 'saying precisely what he thought in the strongest possible language', his reforming zeal, long absences due to sickness in the family and the publication of his unorthodox scholarly views were all detrimental to the success of his legal practice. He died at the age of 54 after a long struggle with tuberculosis.

McLennan made a number of original contributions to contemporary debates on the origins of humanity, and to the emerging discipline of anthropology more generally. His writings drew on classical scholarship, his legal training, and the growing accumulation of ethnographic evidence. Assuming that history spanned some 6,000 years, McLennan initially endorsed the patriarchal theory of human origins. By his mid-thirties, he redirected his attention to the implications of the far longer chronology. McLennan was convinced that 'exotic and savage races' such as Australian Aborigines, described by missionaries and travellers, presented a compelling picture of early humanity, with people human in form only. But savagery could also be seen closer to home, in contemporary London, where one could find 'the lowest incestuous combinations of kindred to the highest group [to which McLennan himself belonged] based on solemn monogamous marriage'. In that centre of arts, industry and intelligence lived 'predatory bands, leading the life of the lowest nomads', some ignorant of marriage; others for whom 'promiscuity is an open, unabashed organization' (McLennan 1869: 542).

McLennan's best-known work, *Primitive Marriage* (1865), is devoted to exploring what happened before the patriarchal past reconstructed from written sources. Since the human species developed so unequally that 'almost every conceivable phase of progress may be studied, as somewhere observed and recorded', McLennan argued, 'the study of races in their primitive condition' was one of two foundational sources of evidence about early forms of human organisation. Borrowing linguistic procedures to analyse social practices rather than texts, he attempted to identify a relic of archaic customary behaviour which was shared by both 'civilised' and 'primitive' peoples. It was the reported widespread practice of female infanticide among contemporary 'savages', together with almost universal incidence of bride capture symbolism in marriage ceremonies, which he identified as the key to reconstructing archaic social arrangements.

McLennan's professional training infused his work. Point by point, he outlined arguments to support his contention that original humans recognised descent from mothers rather than fathers, that primitive hordes practised female infanticide to such an extent that they were compelled to capture grown women from neighbouring hordes for sex and for marriage, and that logical developments of those practices led to their mitigation. Much of his case rested on what would make sense to a 'reasonable man', 'given the facts of human nature', in mid-nineteenth-century Britain. The argument draws on classical jurisprudence, includes Latin citations from Greek and Roman authors, and utilises ethnographic reports on 'primitive' peoples interspersed with historical evidence regarding the Celts in ancient Britain.

McLennan based his theory of sex-selective infanticide, which he believed was universally practised by primitive tribes, on what he took to be the self-evident physical superiority of males. Members of such groups must have felt some sort of primitive fellowships as companions in war or the chase, or joint tenants of the same cave or grove, but had no sense of kinship. As humans developed, they tried to find better ways to adopt to their circumstances:

> To tribes surrounded by enemies, and, unaided by art, contending with the difficulties of subsistence, sons were a source of strength, both for defence and in the quest for food, daughters a source of weakness ... As braves and hunters were required and valued, it would be the interest of every horde to rear, when possible, its healthy male children. It would be less its interest to rear females, as they would be less capable of self-support, and of contributing, by their exertions, to the common good.
>
> *(McLennan 1865: 139, 165; 1896: 76, 90)*

Female infanticide, in turn, left primitive human hordes with very few young women of their own and occasionally with none. To obtain wives in this situation, men had to capture women from adjoining tribes. Over time, the habit of obtaining wives outside one's own group was consolidated into a cultural preference for exogamy and matrilineal descent. As members of one tribe or group married into others, 'blood ties' emerged. These blood ties encouraged reciprocity between groups and cooperation and harmony within groups. With the arrival of settled agriculture and rights in property, infanticide and the scarcity of women gradually abated, each man could be certain of just one wife, and descent and individual inheritance could be worked out with greater precision. As civilisation advanced, the system of kinship through females only was succeeded by one which acknowledged kinship through males also; and which in most cases passed into a system which acknowledged kinship through males only. As soon as that happened, strict patriarchal rule, as described in Maine's *Ancient Law*, was consolidated. As fathers gained authority, it was natural that mothers lost theirs. At the beginning of written history, the *patria potestas* was in most cases so firmly established that fathers had the power of life and death over wives and children, and that these were as devoid of rights as if they had been slaves. All of this, McLennan added, of course referred to 'a period long anterior to that at which humane and reasonable considerations are influential enough to procure for women some approach to an equality of rights' (McLennan 1886: 244–245, note 1).

Lewis Henry Morgan (1818–1881)

Morgan was born in the state of New York, the ninth of thirteen children of a wealthy farmer. The talented lad studied law, and was admitted to the bar in 1842. In his twenties, Morgan helped manage the family farms, and lectured on temperance and on the genius of the Grecian race and their comparison with heroes of the American Revolution. He also spent some time with the Iroquois, pioneering what would later be regarded as ethnographic research. Over the following years, Morgan combined sporadic research and writing on the Iroquois with his increasingly successful legal practice. He eventually retired from business so he could devote his whole time to research. Morgan became one of the most celebrated American scholars of his time and is regarded as the inventor of kinship as a field of research.

Morgan's legal training, his admiration of Greek classical culture and fascination with America's indigenous peoples infused his scholarly writings, and inspired the major insight which guided his work. Morgan was familiar with the wide-ranging significance of what is now called kinship in both civil and canon law. He learnt enough about the Seneca to notice they had a different classificatory system for kin from contemporary Europeans, and read the Classics in enough depth to realise that they too wrote of peoples with unfamiliar ways of reckoning family relationships. In order to gather more information on kinship, Morgan undertook several field trips to the American West, and began to assemble a comprehensive set of the world's kinship nomen-clature systems. The result of this research was a massive four-volume work, *Systems of Consanguinity and Affinity of the Human Family*, published in 1871.

Until his late forties, Morgan took for granted the short Biblical chronology of human origins. Around 1867, he began grappling with the implications of immensely longer human prehistory. His new scheme was outlined in *Ancient Society* (1877). For centuries, Morgan noted, it was thought that 'savage' or 'barbaric' peoples were the result of degeneration of an original society built around monogamous cou-ples and their families. More recently, some American scholars sug-gested that more or less advanced races were the result of separate acts of creation. Rejecting both views, Morgan argued that all humanity originated from a single source, probably diffused by migration from a single centre in Asia. Progressing at varied rates through their 'different but uniform channels', Morgan held, all human groups were bound to pass through the same basic stages: Savagery, Barbarism and Civilisation.

Morgan's contribution to reconstructing the developmental sequence of humanity integrated three forms of scholarship. First, in what was by then commonplace, he argued that current observations of primitive peoples supplied scientific information about the past of humanity. Second, focussing on technologies, systems of production, and forms of inheritance, Morgan integrated modern anthropological observations with extensive classical scholarship. Third, just as languages were believed to preserve in them traces of earlier linguistic forms, Morgan argued that what might be called the grammar of kinship terminology preserved in it, often for centuries, traces of earlier social organisation which existed when the system of consanguinity and affinity was formed.

In reflecting on the motive force behind the successive stages of human development, Morgan drew on his worldly experience. Having participated for a number of years in the cutthroat world of industry and property speculation, he concluded that changes in the arts of subsistence, accelerated by concerns with preserving and augmenting private property, were the only conceivable agencies powerful enough to drive such great and epoch-making changes. In this scenario, ascending stages of barbarism and civilisation were associated with increasingly complex forms of technology and refined forms of marriage. Transformation of one stage to another was driven by major inventions and discoveries. This progress was made complex through the sharing of technologies between different tribes, and the uneven advance or decadence of specific peoples. Eventually, just one people – the Aryan race – rose to the fore.

Advancing stages of technological development were associated with five major ascending forms of marriage. The patriarchal family, characteristic of pastoral peoples and posited by generations of scholars as the original and universal human institution, only emerged in the fourth stage of development. In contrast to other scholars attempting to reconstruct the long chronology, Morgan relegated the Hebrew and Roman forms of patriarchal family to an exceptional stage of development, with limited influence upon the human race. This difference aside, Morgan's description of the institution itself was close to that of Maine. The patriarchal family of the Roman type, Morgan (1907 [1877]: 465–467) believed, had little to recommend it; not least since 'paternal authority passed beyond the bounds of reason into an excess of domination'.

It was the 'Monogamian Family', founded upon marriage between single pairs, with an exclusive cohabitation, which constituted the final, and most significant form of domestic institution. Despite its many positive features, Morgan believed that even this family form could be made better. Despising the 'greed for gain' he saw all around him, he hoped that the next stage of human development would go beyond a preoccupation with property. Perhaps the best-known use of Morgan's work was in the later writings of Marx and Engels.

Karl Marx (1818–1883)

Karl Marx was born into a middle-class Jewish family in Prussia. His father insisted that Karl study law in order to secure a comfortable livelihood. Marx enrolled at the University of Bonn, transferred to the University of Berlin, and eventually submitted a doctoral dissertation at the University of Jena. To the despair of his parents, Karl lived beyond his means, took part in rowdy escapades, drank too much beer and earned a reputation for philosophical radicalism. This closed off chances of a career in the Prussian bureaucracy, a university post, or even legal practice. In 1843, against opposition from both families, Marx married the educated daughter of a Prussian baron. The couple lived in more or less genteel poverty punctuated by periods of severe ill health and family tragedy; only three of their seven children survived to adulthood. Marx became one of the leading radical intellectuals of his age.

When Marx arrived at the University of Berlin, the Faculty of Law was a ferment of intellectual life. All his university teachers were accomplished exponents of a systematising approach to civil law based on the *Pandects*. Marx himself set out to translate the *Pandects* into German, and began writing a treatise on Roman law. While he soon embarked on quite different projects, Marx continued to use his detailed knowledge of classical antiquity as a rich comparative source of social arrangements. His concept of alienation, for example, drew on both Hegelian and Roman legal sources. In ancient Rome, which continued to be Marx's principal model, 'alienation of domain' related specifically to the transfer, surrender or loss of patrimony. Such expropriation was among the most bitterly resented abuses of rulers' powers. Among the destructive consequences of effects of *alienatio* were the loss of (men's) identity, of citizenship, and, indeed, of the entire basis for social belonging (Kelley 1984: 259). In effect, the Roman concept of *alienatio* referred to a thorough destruction of all aspects of patriarchal power. More widely, Marx's training in jurisprudence provided him with an appreciation of the extensive influence of Roman law in European history.

In the last years of his life, when he was battling debilitating ill health, Marx took up systematic study of the emerging discipline of anthropology. In his *Ethnological Notebooks*, he began a systematic study of authors dealing with early human institutions, and moved from speculation about generic human beings to consideration of the historical variability of ancient peoples (Krader 1974: 5, 85). The most extensive passages in the *Notebooks* are taken up with excerpts from Morgan and vehement critiques of Maine. Morgan provided Marx with evidence that a form of matrilineal primitive communism preceded societies built around private property and subordination of women. This meant that neither property nor male domination had any foundation in what philosophical and legal anthropology had regarded as natural law (Kelley 1984: 258–259). It also proved that

Maine was wrong to replace such natural law by notions of a primordial and gradually evolving patriarchal society. Throughout the *Notebooks*, Marx presents what is in effect a sophisticated critique of the then commonplace notion that contemporary 'primitive' people resembled the barbaric childhood of humanity. Quite the contrary: prepatriarchal societies, he speculated, might well provide a model for a future communist society. After his death, Marx's lifelong collaborator Frederick Engels drew on the *Ethnological Notebooks* to write a book which later provided a key inspiration to second-wave feminists.

Friedrich Engels (1820–1895)

Friedrich Engels, the eldest son of a successful German industrialist, was born in Prussia in 1820. Engels never finished his formal education, but attended some university lectures in Berlin when stationed there as a soldier. At the age of 22, he was sent to work for a Manchester textile firm in which his father was a major shareholder. Engels' observations of what was then one of the most dynamic centres of industrial production provided the basis of a searing critique of capitalist society. *The Condition of the Working Class in England* (1844) contained a detailed account of workers' desperate living conditions, the harshness and degradation of factory labour, and the organisation of capitalist industry. The work was made possible through the assistance of Mary Burns, a young Irish working woman who showed Engels around Manchester and introduced him to local workers and activists. Engels and Burns became lifelong partners but never married, in part because both strenuously opposed the institution of marriage. After a long meeting with Karl Marx in 1844, the two young men cemented a productive friendship that would last for the rest of their lives.

Engels' *The Origin of the Family, Private Property and the State, in Light of the Researches of Lewis H. Morgan* (1884) drew on Marx's ethnological notebooks to chart the whole span of human development from primitive communities to modern families. While to Morgan the patriarchal family of the Hebrews and Romans was an exceptional case in the evolution of humanity, Engels, reverted to the more common unilineal scheme and argued that all societies went through a patriarchal stage.

At its best, *The Origin of the Family, Private Property and the State* extends Engels' and Marx's earlier insights into women's oppression under contemporary capitalism, and sharpens what Engels believed was a fundamental revolutionary insight: namely, Morgan's rediscovery 'of the precedence of the matriarchal over the patriarchal gens'. The text of the book reflects its hybrid origins. In between energetic descriptions of the customs of a bewildering variety of people in different places and times are witty and sarcastic comments, angry denunciations, rousing revolutionary insights, and detailed theoretical polemics on interpretations of classical texts. Engels' disdain of loveless bourgeois marriages provided the backbone of the book's narrative. Rather than portray the development from matriarchy to patriarchy and the bourgeois nuclear family as a journey of progress, the book depicted it as a story of wasted potential and enslavement of women. One of the most absurd notions taken over from the eighteenth-century Enlightenment, Engels noted, is that in the beginning of society woman was the slave of man. On the contrary, he argued, 'among all the savages and barbarians of the lower and middle stages … the position of women is not only free, but honourable' (Engels 1972 [1884]: 113). Engels believed that early matriarchal societies, characterised by mother right and matrilineality, were egalitarian, primitive communist communities. Women were charged with household production and men with fighting, hunting and fishing, but both were equally valued.

As the means of production developed, division of labour became more complex, and people became capable of producing more than was necessary to satisfy their immediate needs. The emergence of private property and class society was linked to the triumph of patriarchy:

> The overthrow of mother right was the *world historical defeat of the female sex*. The man took command in the home also; the woman was degraded and reduced to servitude; she became the slave of his lust and a mere instrument for the production of children … With the patriarchal family we enter the field of written history and class conflict.
> *(Engels 1972 [1884]: 120–121)*

Marx and Engels both believed (as did Maine) that the slave-holding patriarchal household encapsulated in it later forms of exploitative social relations:

[it contained] in germ not only slavery (*servitus*) but also serfdom, since from the beginning it is related to agricultural services. It contains in miniature all the contradictions which later extend throughout society and its state.

(Engels 1972 [1884]: 121–122)

But while Maine, Bachofen, McLennan and Morgan all saw the history of family forms as a tale of gradual improvement, Engels depicted the same developments as both an improvement and a deterioration of social conditions. As he put it:

The modern individual family is founded on the open or concealed domestic slavery of the wife, and ... modern society is a mass composed of these individual families as its molecules ... In the great majority of cases today, at least in the possessing classes, the husband is obliged to earn a living and support his family, and that in itself gives him a position of supremacy without any need for special legal titles and privileges. Within the family he is the bourgeois, and the wife represents the proletariat.

(Engels 1972 [1884]: 136–137)

Rather than the height of civilisation, or the pinnacle of progress from status to contract, women's position in bourgeois family could be compared to prostitution; among the proletarians, unremitting wage labour of all family members destroyed most vestiges of family life and prepared the way for renewed relations between women and men based on love rather than exploitation. However, while the whole book is dedicated to demonstrating how families oppress women, Engels reserved the term 'patriarchal family' to what he saw as a crucial, but long past, intermediate stage in a unilineal development of a core human institution.

In time, *The Origin of the Family, Private Property and the State* became fossilised as a socialist classic, and was for decades taught in Eastern Europe as a factually accurate account of early human development. As Lenin put it in a lecture delivered at the Sverdlovsk University in 1919, 'This is one of the fundamental works of modern socialism, every sentence of which can be accepted with confidence, in the assurance that it has not been said at random but is based on immense historical and political material.' In the late 1960s, the book was rediscovered by Western feminists; the questions it raised and the territory it mapped stimulated several decades of feminist scholarship. While Engels' *Origin* influenced *second-wave* feminism, it was his contemporary August Bebel whose work affected women's movements at the end of the nineteenth century.

August Bebel (1840–1913)

The son of a Prussian non-commissioned officer, August Bebel grew up in extreme poverty. By the time he was thirteen, his father, mother and stepfather had died of tuberculosis. Bebel completed an apprenticeship as a turner and travelled as a journeyman throughout Germany and Austria. In 1860, he established a wood-turning business and began his political career. Shrewd and charismatic, in 1867 Bebel became the first workers' representative elected to the constituent Reichstag of the North German Confederation, a position he held almost continuously until his death. Bebel repeatedly fell foul of state regulations in one of the most repressive regimes in Europe, and spent intermittently almost five years in prison. The months of enforced idleness helped Bebel recover from tuberculosis and provided him with the leisure to draft and revise what would become one of the most influential contemporary feminist texts.

Bebel's aim was to use accounts of ancient matriarchy and patriarchy in a compelling programme of social transformation led by the German socialist party. Looking deep into the past was important in countering arguments that women's position could not be changed, because it had been the same from time immemorial. The fact of matriarchal past, as established by scholars such as Bachofen, Morgan and McLennan and later systematised by Engels, provided indisputable proof that women's character and relations with men varied over time, and could again be fundamentally changed.

Bebel's publications reflected his skills as a public speaker. His underlying argument was that women's equality and socialism were of necessity linked. To make his case, Bebel presented a vast range of evidence beginning with early humanity, spanning classical and medieval history, the Reformation, eighteenth-century Europe and nineteenth-century Germany. In the conclusion, Bebel outlined his vision of a better future: a wholesome and caring heterosexual society where human impulses and talents were not restrained by prejudice, private property and exploitative social regulation, people ate healthy balanced diets, and housework was made easier. Some ingenious gadgets could clean shoes and houses and cook nutritious meals, other inventions would make rain in glasshouses, and prevent the exhaustion of farmland.

An initial primitive communist society ruled by women was an essential part of Bebel's narrative. While production of the necessities of life was at its lowest stage of development, and destined to satisfy only the simplest demands, the activities of men and women were essentially the same. Even in the more sophisticated stage of development preceding patriarchy, described by classical authors as existing among the foreign peoples they encountered:

> 'Matrimonium' was spoken of instead of 'patrimonium', 'mater familias' was said instead of 'pater familias', and one's native country was referred to as the motherland ... Woman was the leader and ruler in this kinship organization and was highly respected, her opinion counting for much in the household as well as in the affairs of the tribe. She is peacemaker and judge, and discharges the duties of religious worship as priestess.
>
> *(Bebel 1910 [1879])*

With more complicated forms of production and increasing division of labour, there emerged forms of specialised skills and knowledge, and these became the province of the men. As a result, men became owners of new sources of wealth. As they accumulated property, men developed an interest in leaving inheritance to their own children. To make sure they knew who these children were, they forced women into monogamy. With dissolution of the old communal organisation and the rise of private property, the power and influence of women declined: 'The matriarchate implied communism and equality of all. The rise of the patriarchate implied the rule of private property and the subjugation and enslavement of woman.' While Engels thought that the change from matriarchate to patriarchate occurred peacefully, Bebel agreed with those who believed it was accompanied by armed conflict. Gradually, the state came into existence as a result of the necessity to regulate, conduct, arbitrate, protect and punish. As legal relations became more and more complex, a special class of persons arose, devoted exclusively to the study of law and having a special interest in complicating the laws still further. This process found its most classic expression in the Roman state, and that explains the influence exerted by Roman law down to the present time.

In Bebel's lifetime, *Women and Socialism* appeared in fifty-three German language editions, was translated into twenty other languages, sold almost a million and a half copies, and formed the basis of countless feminist lectures.

★ ★ ★

Engels' *Origins* and Bebel's *Women and Socialism* demonstrate the key role of nineteenth-century notions of matriarchy and patriarchy, derived in part from classical scholarship, in programmatic schemes of communist revolution, women's emancipation, and socialist future. Many of the same conceptual building blocks came to be employed in a project which challenged mastery in quite different ways, by revolutionising the understanding of human psychology. 'The ego', Freud summarised his psychoanalytic theories, 'is not master in its own house'.

Sigmund Freud (1856–1939)

Sigmund Freud was born in Moravia into a large Jewish family. When he was four, the family moved to Vienna, Freud's home for most of the rest of his life. The talented young scholar attended prestigious municipal classical schools; one of his final matriculation examinations was based on a passage, in Greek, from Sophocles' *Oedipus Rex*, Freud briefly studied philosophy and later majored in zoology in the medical school of the University of Vienna. By the age of twenty-five he had become an accomplished zoological researcher and qualified for a doctorate of medicine. Needing a secure income – not least so he could marry – Freud reluctantly decided to become a physician. Over several years, he built up a private practice, fathered six children, developed his interest in psychology, and gradually laid the foundations of what he began to call psychoanalysis.

The core of Freud's approach was his growing conviction that psychological disturbances in later life had their roots in traumatic (male) childhood experiences. In describing the most pivotal of these traumas, Freud reached for the classical authors taught and examined in his academic high school. To most students of psychoanalysis today, the primal Oedipal drama which is at the core of individual psychological development is a rich symbolic device drawing on the work of the ancient Greek playwright Sophocles. Less well known – or treated with some embarrassment and discounted – is Freud's increasing conviction that the story of Oedipus represented actual murderous events in primeval human history: namely, the overthrow of a tyrannical patriarchy.

By the early twentieth century, most anthropologists had abandoned the influential theory of unilineal human development, as well as the less-known argument that this history was to some extent physically recapitulated in the early development of each individual. Published in 1939, Freud's final book restated the same themes with fierce conviction. The narrative theme of *Moses and Monotheism* is a story about Moses, his probable Egyptian origins, his parricide by his Jewish followers, the collective repression and then forgetting of this murder, yet also its survival in the 'collective unconscious' and its later reappearance in religious phenomena. Throughout the text, Freud takes it as read that the Oedipal drama in the early life of each individual in some way recapitulates events in the early history of humanity. Drawing on Darwin, Freud hypothesised that early humans initially lived in small hordes, each dominated by a single older male who governed by brute force, appropriated all the females and brutalised or killed all the young males, including his own sons. Eventually, Freud argued, the sons who had been driven out of the father's horde and lived together in a community rebelled, overpowered the patriarch and together consumed his body. This was the Oedipal drama. In order to be able to live in peace with one another, the victorious brothers formed a social contract of sorts. Each renounced the ideal of gaining for himself the position of father and of possessing his mother or sister: they all agreed to practise exogamy and to avoid incest. As a consequence of the brothers' renunciation of power, a good part of the might previously wielded by the patriarch passed to the women: the father's broken power was replaced by matriarchal regulation of families. During this whole period, sons retained their complex feelings of hatred, fear and reverence of the father. In his place, they declared a certain animal a totem, worshipping it for most of the year and consuming its flesh during designated feast days. Later still, 'a great social revolution' took place. Matriarchy was followed by a restitution of a patriarchal order. However, the new patriarchs never succeeded to the omnipotence of the primeval father. There were too many of them and they lived in larger communities than the original horde; they had to get on with one another and were restricted by social institutions. Thirty-five years after Freud's defiant defence of his last book, Juliet Mitchell employed some of the same arguments in *Psychoanalysis and Feminism*. By the 1990s, similar themes were incorporated into a popular men's mythopoetic movement.

Notes

1 Other ancient civilisations employed different – and usually far longer – chronologies and calendars.
2 The late twentieth century has seen a resurgence of creationist organisations which energetically dispute such claims. See for example Creation Ministries International, http://creation.com/; Answers in Genesis, www.answersingenesis.org/; www.creationevidence.org/about_us/about_creation_evidence_museum_texas.php; and https://creationmuseum.org/creation-science/.

References

Bachofen, Johann Jakob (1992) *Myth, Religion, and Mother Right: Selected writings of Johann Jakob Bachofen*. Translated by Ralph Manheim. Princeton, NJ: Princeton University Press.

Bebel, August (1910 [1879]) *Woman and Socialism*. Jubilee 50th edn. New York: Socialist Literature Company. Transcribed for marxists.org by Andy Blunden. CopyLeft: Creative Commons (Attribute & ShareAlike) marxists.org, 2005.

Diop, Cheikh Anta (1959) *The Cultural Unity of Black Africa: The domains of matriarchy and patriarchy in classical Antiquity*. Chicago, IL: Third World Press.

Engels, Friedrich (1972 [1884]). *The Origin of the Family, Private Property and the State, in Light of the Researches of Lewis H. Morgan*. Reprint, with an introduction and notes by Eleanor Burke Leacock. Translated by Alec West. New York: International Publishers.

Engels, Friedrich (1987 [1844]) *The Condition of the Working Class in England*. Harmondsworth: Penguin.

Freud, Sigmund (1939) *Moses and Monotheism*. New York: A. A. Knopf.

Kelley, Donald R. (1984) 'The Science of Anthropology: An essay on the very old Marx', *Journal of the History of Ideas* 45(2): 245–262.

Krader, Lawrence (ed.) (1974) *The Ethnological Notebooks of Karl Marx*, 2nd edn. Assen, The Netherlands: Van Gorcum.

Maine, Sir Henry James Sumner (1917 [1861]) *Ancient Law: Its connection to the history of early society*. London: Dent. Project Gutenberg eBook, accessed 7 October 2007 [eBook #22910], www.gutenberg.org/files/22910/22910-h/22910-h.htm.

McLennan, John Ferguson (1865) *Primitive Marriage. An inquiry into the origin of the form of capture in marriage ceremonies*. Edinburgh: Adam and Charles Black. www.archive.org/details/cu31924101874190.

McLennan, John Ferguson (1869) 'The Early History of Man', *Northern British Review* 50(1): 516–549.

McLennan, John Ferguson (1886) *Studies in Ancient History, Comprising a Reprint of Primitive Marriage: An inquiry into the origin of the form of capture in marriage ceremonies*. London: Macmillan.

McLennan, John Ferguson (1896) *Studies in Ancient History. The second series. Comprising an Inquiry into the Origin of Exogamy. By the late John Ferguson McLennan, edited by his widow (Eleonora Anne McLelland) and Arthur Platt*. London: Macmillan. www.archive.org/details/studiesinancient00mcleuoft.

Morgan, Lewis Henry (1871) *Systems of Consanguinity and Affinity of the Human Family*. Washington, DC: Smithsonian Institution.

Morgan, Lewis Henry (1907 [1877]) *Ancient Society: Researches in the lines of human progress from savagery through barbarism to civilization*. New York: Henry Holt. Digitised copy, www.archive.org/details/ancientsociety00morggoog.

von Schiller, Friedrich (1972 [1789]) 'The Nature and Value of Universal History', *History and Theory* 11(3): 321–334.

5

PATRIARCHY AND THE MAKING OF SISTERHOOD

It has been a strength of patriarchy in all its historic forms to assimilate itself so perfectly to socioeconomic, political, and cultural structures as to be virtually invisible. Now that it is no longer hidden from view, ours may be an historical moment when those relations are in sufficient conflict for us not only to 'see' how the patriarchal system works, but also to act with that vision so as to put an end to it.

(Kelly 1979: 225)

In countries of the global North, the late 1960s and early 1970s saw the invigoration and rise of new social movements with their vibrant optimism and belief that utopian dreams could come true and profound social change was just around the corner. Wherever activists looked, possibilities opened up by economic prosperity came up against oppressive institutions, ponderous bureaucracies, stifling conventions and unjust wars. For a decade or more, millions of people were swept up in the wave of reforming energy, protesting involvement in the Vietnam War, debating private lives and social alternatives, and setting up new social arrangements. In order to unite people grappling with a broad range of problems and flawed institutions, New Left activists coined a deliberately vague term: 'the System', to describe a common enemy (see McCann and Szalay 2005).

During the same period, families everywhere seemed to lurch into crisis. Changing economies, women's improved educational qualifications and early successes of equal rights campaigns increased women's participation in the workforce and expanded their capacity to set up independent households. Several years before new forms of contraception became available, fertility rates had already begun to fall. Ideologies of domesticity and conventions built around male breadwinner families made less and less sense. Children and wives challenged authoritarian fathers. The easing of restrictions on divorce and greater expectations for married life saw divorce – and remarriage – rates soar. Many radicals welcomed what they saw as the death throes of a deeply flawed institution; conservatives began organising to shore up traditional families.

As Kelly noted in the opening quote of this chapter, with the resurgence of popular radicalism the concept of patriarchy resurfaced into the glare of public debate. This time, it was as one of the core organising concepts of a vibrant social movement contesting women's oppression. For many feminists, 'the Patriarchy' became a gendered version of 'the System'. As one US women's liberation activist put it, while many women see 'the System as the sole enemy, others point out that men cannot get off that easily, since they created the System and preserve it' (Morgan 1970: xviii). Later commentators often suggest that this all-encompassing meaning of patriarchy was taken up in proportion to the growth of feminist consciousness: the stronger one's feminism, the more extensive and principled use of the concept. Two decades later, the story goes, as feminist scholarship became more sophisticated, patriarchy became less effective as a conceptual and political tool.

What happened at the time was more complicated and uneven. Patriarchy meant different things to different feminist activists, and was employed in different – and sometimes incompatible – projects. In some texts, patriarchy is all but timeless; in others, it represents a particular, historically specific form of social relations. Some accounts of patriarchy give centre stage to men's wilful sexism, others depict it as an inexorable, machine-like structure, operating according to its own logic and laws. Some writers locate patriarchy in habits of mind, others in relations of production. Some writers outline sweeping global histories of women's oppression, others call for careful attention to racial discrimination, different groups, times and places, and caution when using historically bound categories of analysis (see for example Davis 1976). And while some activists could not imagine a women's movement without the concept of patriarchy, others reserved the term for a limited number of past societies, or mounted sophisticated critiques of its use. This diversity was not random. Although Western feminists confronted similar problems, they were deeply affected by local issues, ways of seeing, and distinct academic traditions. A history of civil rights struggles, emphasis on constitutional guarantees and engagement with psychological issues in the US, for example, differed markedly from the socialist and union tradition and emphasis on workers' rights in the UK.

Two early second-wave feminist texts published in the US exemplified thinking with patriarchy as an all-encompassing system. One written by the sculptor and literary scholar Kate Millett and the other by the accomplished poet Adrienne Rich, both books saw patriarchy as an all-powerful institution stemming from habits of mind. The books synthesised powerful streams of current feminist wisdom and proved immensely popular and influential. They also exasperated large numbers of feminists who were brought up to analyse core social divisions and inequalities with more precise intellectual tools.

Millett's *Sexual Politics* (1970) is regarded by many commentators as a classic statement of radical feminist theory. By the time the book was published in 1970, Millett was 35 years old, an established sculptor, literary scholar and feminist activist. The book, which was first written as a PhD thesis in comparative literature at Columbia University, combines Millett's searing wit, political commitment and professional expertise as a literary critic. It covers a remarkable breadth of material, and was completed in remarkably short time.[1]

Most of *Sexual Politics* deals with the historical background of contemporary sexual arrangements and with the whole corpus of work of four influential contemporary writers: D. H. Lawrence, Henry Miller, Norman Mailer and Jean Genet. The vast range of material is held together by a powerful guiding thread. Patriarchy, Millett argues, stems above all from habits of mind: 'So deeply embedded is patriarchy that the character structure it creates in both sexes is perhaps even more a habit of mind and a way of life than a political system'. In turn, such habits of mind, forming an often invisible substructure of human consciousness, can be studied through their reflections in the works of great writers. This core argument is elaborated in a 36-page theory chapter.

The chapter begins with broadening of the term 'politics' to all structured relationships of power, as well as stratagems designed to maintain such systems. Patriarchal government, then, is an institution whereby that half of the populace which is female is controlled by that which is male. Our society, like all other historical civilisations, is a patriarchy (even though it exhibits a great variety of local and historical forms). While most of her argument concerns relations between women and men, Millett includes both gender and age in her definition of patriarchy: its basic principles, she posits, are twofold: 'male shall dominate female, elder male shall dominate younger'. The bulk of the chapter is devoted to outlining the main features of patriarchy and the mechanisms which perpetuate them. Of necessity, the material is derivative and schematic, not least because it includes just about everything: ideology, biology, sociology, political economy, economics, education, violence, anthropology, myth, religion and psychology.

In patriarchy, Millet notes, consent is manufactured through socialisation of both sexes to temperament, sex-role and status privileging males and subordinating females. The roles and attributes allotted to females are closest to the biological and those for males to truly human or cultural spheres. While it cannot be ruled out that some aspects of male and female status, role and temperament are biologically based, profound gender differences are established through conditioning in early childhood, and then self-perpetuated through the activity of people who learn to see them as natural and necessary. Patriarchy's chief institution, the family, is an anomalous feudal-like institution in democratic societies. While socialisation is the key engine of perpetuating patriarchy, economic and educational factors – and brute force – are important as well. Importantly, in an argument repeated by many other feminist writers, Millett claims that:

> under patriarchy the female did not herself develop the symbols by which she is described. As both the primitive and the civilised worlds are male worlds, the ideas which shaped culture in regard to the female were also of male design.

Millett concludes the section on force with a sweeping statement containing, as a later feminist critic put it, a hodgepodge of examples illustrating patriarchal violence towards women:

> The history of patriarchy presents a variety of cruelties and barbarities: the suttee execution in India, the crippling deformity of footbinding in China, the lifelong ignominy of the veil in Islam, or the widespread persecution of sequestration, the gynacium, and purdah. Phenomena such as clitoridectomy, clitoral incision, the sale and enslavement of women under one guise or another, involuntary and child marriages, concubinage and prostitution, still take place – the first in Africa, the latter in the Near and Far East, the last generally.
>
> *(Millett 1970: 47)*

Millett has often been accused of ignoring social structures to focus on surface ideological phenomena. Yet there is nothing accidental in her emphasis. Millett uses historical analysis to deliberately reverse conventional Marxist understanding of base and superstructure. To her, psychic structures constitute the bedrock of patriarchal social relations, while policies, laws, economies and education systems are parts of the superstructure. The failure of attempts to liberate women in early revolutionary Russia is a case in point. The Marxist theory which guided the revolution had failed to supply a sufficient ideological base for a sexual revolution, and was remarkably naive as to the historical and psychological strength of patriarchy. Since habits of mind constitute the bedrock of patriarchy, Millett's programmatic conclusion is that in order for a just society to emerge, the family, as that term is presently understood, must go. Only a sexual revolution would bring the institution of patriarchy to an end, abolishing both the ideology of male supremacy and the traditional socialisation by which it is upheld in matters of status, role and temperament.

Published in 1976, Rich's *Of Woman Born: Motherhood as Experience and Institution* was an eloquent and influential restatement of what, by now, was identified as radical feminist theory. The daughter and granddaughter of privileged and idiosyncratic Jewish intellectuals from the American South, Adrienne Rich was 43 when she started writing the book. An acclaimed poet, academic and feminist activist, she was also the mother of three teenage sons, an eminent figure who publicly reflected, in her poetry, on the dissolution of her marriage, the recent suicide of her husband, and her growing passionate love of women.

While Millett discerned the contours of patriarchy in the works of leading male writers, Rich thought deeply about the experience of motherhood in order to uncover traces of patriarchy in her own life. She too set her reflections against a vast historical canvas. Her book is built around a tension between two meanings of motherhood. One is powerful, potentially liberating, affirming and awe-inspiring; the other caged, corrupted and degraded by patriarchy. In defining the institution of patriarchy, Rich acknowledged that women's lives vary, and societies are not all the same. Under patriarchy, she wrote:

> I may live in purdah or drive a truck; I may raise my children on a kibbutz or be the sole breadwinner for a fatherless family or participate in a demonstration against abortion legislation with my baby on my back; I may work as a 'barefoot doctor' in a village commune in the People's Republic of China, or make my life on a lesbian commune in New England; I may become a hereditary or elected head of state or wash the underwear of a millionaire's wife; I may serve my husband his early-morning coffee within the clay walls of a Berber village or march in an academic procession; whatever my status or situation, my derived economic class, or my sexual preference, I live under the power of the fathers, and I have access only to so much of privilege or influence as the patriarchy is willing to accede to me, and only for so long as I will pay the price for male approval.
>
> *(Rich 1976: 58)*

Beneath the vast diversity of individual lives, Rich believed, lay a multidimensional and omnipresent cross-cultural, global power of men over women: 'the core of all power relationships, a tangle of lust, violence, possession, fear, conscious longing, unconscious hostility, sentiment, rationalisation: the sexual understructure of social and political forms'. This power has been difficult to grasp because it 'permeates everything, even the language in which we try to describe it. It is diffuse and concrete; symbolic and literal; universal, and expressed with local variations which obscure its universality'. Patriarchy, then, could be defined as:

> a familial-social, ideological, political system in which men – by force, direct pressure, or through ritual, tradition, law, and language, customs, etiquette, education, and the division of labor, determine what part women shall or shall not play, and in which the female is everywhere subsumed under the male.
>
> *(Rich 1976: 57)*

Like Millett, Rich believed that the family reproduced patriarchy from one generation to the next. In a passage which draws on Simone de Beauvoir, and beyond her on Morgan, Bachofen and Engels, Rich argues that the individual patriarchal family unit originated with the idea of sexual possession, property and the desire to see one's property transmitted to one's biological descendants. In turn, the creation of the patriarchal family deformed the quintessential human unit, the mother–child relationship. This had devastating consequences for 'woman' whose full meaning and capacity is domesticated and confined within strictly defined limits. Even the female generative organs, the matrix of human life, have become a prime target of patriarchal technology. Equally tragic is the fact that women, in their role as mothers, play a crucial role in preparing their children to enter the 'the patriarchal system', and to perpetuate it in their own turn. The book concludes by calling on women to repossess their own bodies, and thus help dismantle patriarchy.

The theologian Mary Daly arrived at similar conclusions from yet another starting point. Educated in Catholic schools, Daly received her first PhD in the US in 1954. Over the next ten years she gained two more doctorates – in theology and philosophy – from the University of Fribourg in Switzerland. In 1966 she was appointed a member of the Theology Department of the then all-male Boston College. Daly's first feminist book, *The Church and the Second Sex* (1968), was written from the standpoint of a devout Christian woman proposing church reform. A scholarly overview of misogyny in the Catholic Church from the time of the early Fathers to the present, both as represented in the Bible and in organisational Church practices, the book proposed a number of practical reforms which would allow women to make a positive contribution to the faith. These included the ordination of women, allowing nuns open access to the community, and analysis and reform of male-dominated theological concepts. Soon after its publication, *The Church and the Second Sex* was described by a (male) Harvard professor of Roman Catholic studies as 'the most sophisticated, the most progressive, and the most honest of all the works that have attempted to deal with women in the church' (cited in Braude 2006: 375).

Controversy surrounding the book's publication (including attempts to sack the theologian from her job), contributed to Daly's transformation from a reformist Catholic to a post-Christian radical feminist. In her next book, *Beyond God the Father* (1973), Daly challenged the whole edifice of patriarchal religion ('Mary Daly' 2004; Hoagland and Frye 2000). From an earnest theologian, she gradually became a transgressive, in-your-face radical feminist, inventing new words and making fun of both the church establishment and feminist academics. Her book *Gyn/Ecology: The Metaethics of Radical Feminism* (1978), provided a grand overview of the psychological and physical destruction of women across continents and centuries by practices such as Indian suttee, Chinese footbinding, African genital mutilation, European witch burning and American gynaecology. Accused by feminist critics of essentialism (or treating concepts like rocks rather than made-up, changing human products), she began to call herself a quintessentialist, and named her next book *Quintessence* (1998). While Daly's later work parted company with many other Christian feminists, she continued to inspire their efforts to recast the patriarchal elements of Christian theology (see for example Braude 2004; 2006; Coakley 2013).

Freud, psychoanalysis and habits of mind

In the work of Millett and Rich, patriarchy was conceptualised as a powerful underlying 'system' perpetuated above all through transhistorical habits of mind, and built into a whole range of institutions which helped enforce and reproduce it. For both writers, the family played a key role in socialising babies into a patriarchal mentality which was then reinforced by various other socialisation agencies. In dealing with this process, most feminists simply reached for the sort of behaviourist psychology used in everyday conversations and popular books. A minority went further, and attempted to ground patriarchy in more complex theorisations. Sigmund Freud's work was one obvious starting point. Certainly, many feminists rejected psychoanalysis as sexist. Others went to great lengths to separate the potential of Freud's work from the repressive way it was practised. In Anglophone countries, two of the best-known attempts to do so were made by the British socialist feminist Juliet Mitchell and the American anthropologist Gayle Rubin. While Mitchell believed that her approach provided the basis for powerful theorisation of patriarchy, Rubin deliberately avoided using the term.

Steeped in contemporary feminist and anthropological debates, both Mitchell and Rubin drew on the work of Freud and three influential French theoreticians to tackle the same basic puzzle: how are kinship rules which disadvantage women transmitted from generation to generation as ingrained habits of mind? The Marxist theorist Louis Althusser supplied a theorisation of ideology, or the specific ways of thinking and 'ideological apparatuses' anchored in different ways of organising production. The anthropologist Claude Lévi-Strauss contributed speculation that human culture and social organisation were built up through gifts and reciprocity, and cemented through men's exchange of women. Finally, the psychoanalyst Jacques Lacan argued that children's entry into culture through the acquisition of language produced fundamental differences in the structure of the unconscious between women and men, determined by having or not possessing the *phallus*, the symbolic attribute of powerful maleness. As Mitchell later put it, even though most feminist scholars later focussed on his linguistic theory, she wanted to 'hijack Lacan for an anthropology of the family' (Mitchell 2000: xxix).

Juliet Mitchell was born in New Zealand in 1940. In the 1960s she combined work as a lecturer in literature at two English universities with New Left activism. In 1966 Mitchell published an influential overview article, 'Women: The Longest Revolution'. Five years later she elaborated the same themes *in Woman's Estate*, a socialist feminist classic which was eventually translated into eighteen languages and is still in print. In 1968 Mitchell set out to write a socialist feminist text on the twentieth-century Western family. By the time she finished what became *Psychoanalysis and Feminism*, Mitchell was hooked on Freud.

Just as for Millett and Rich, Mitchell's intellectual project was grounded in a fundamental strategic puzzle: what, despite enormous social, economic, legal progress, accounts for the conservative undertow that sooner or later confronts all projects of gender equality? Certainly, some of the support for the *status quo* stemmed from socialisation and choice. However, Mitchell believed that there also seemed to be something that persists which is incommensurate with the real social situation, and which structures sexual difference and the inequalities that always arise from it, despite the enormous diversity of social practice. Freud's account, she concluded, opened the way to understanding this inherent conservatism and the transmission of unconscious ideas and effects of sexual difference which reproduced it from one generation to the next.

In relying on Freud, Mitchell did not reject Marxism, and indeed still sees herself as a Marxist. The new theorisation of patriarchy (understood here as the specific rule of fathers, rather than the more general sexism of men) would not replace analyses of productive social relations, but stand alongside them. The economic mode of capitalism would be analysed using Marxist theoretical tools; the ideological mode of patriarchy using Freudian ones (Mitchell 1975: 412).

Most of *Psychoanalysis and Feminism* is given over to a careful exposition of Freud's theories. The implications of this work for women's liberation are spelt out in two brief concluding chapters, which rely heavily on Freud's final and most controversial books, *Totem and Taboo* (1913) and *Moses and Monotheism* (1939). In essence, Mitchell argues, the primal crime (the sons' murder of the powerful father who kept all women of the tribe to himself) followed by the brothers' guilt and agreement to peaceably share and exchange the women among themselves, constitutes the beginnings of social law and of morality. From then on, the history of the primal crime and the cultural laws it gave rise to live on in each man's unconscious, and are transmitted from generation to generation through the mechanism of the Oedipus complex.

In this scheme, women's role in the foundation of civilisation is quite unlike that of their brothers: men exchange women, women are the objects of men's exchange. Certainly, there are substantial differences between different societies. Yet in relation to the law of the father the position of all women is fundamentally similar. This means that the liberation of women through changing – even revolutionising – ideas and social relations, whether by consent or by violence, can never be ultimately successful. As summarised in a well-known defence of Mitchell's work:

> From a feminist reading of anthropology we learned that the social meaning of maleness and femaleness is constructed through kinship rules which prescribe patterns of sexual dominance and subordination. From psychoanalysis we learned how these kinship rules become inscribed on the unconscious psyche of the female child via the traumatic re-orientation of sexual desire within the Oedipal phase away from the mother and towards the father ... the two arguments combined ... provide a powerful account of the 'generation of a patriarchal system that must by definition oppress women'.
>
> *(Alexander and Taylor 1981: 370–371)*

So is patriarchy here to stay? With the passage of time, Mitchell suggests, the unconscious patriarchal law has developed an increasingly tangible internal contradiction that might lead to its demise. In particular, the deep structure of nuclear family – 'the modern form of the exchange of women and the taboo on incest' – has come into increasing conflict with capitalist social relations and the organisation of work. It follows that 'women have to organize themselves as a group to effect a change in the basic ideology of human society'. Patriarchy can then be somehow defeated through a 'struggle based on a theory of the social non-necessity at this stage of development of the laws instituted by patriarchy' (Mitchell 1975: 414).

When she wrote *Psychoanalysis and Feminism*, Mitchell was a well-known and influential author and activist. A much younger Gayle Rubin began grappling with similar issues and theorists as an undergraduate student in a progressive American university. What eventually became 'The Traffic in Women: Notes on the "Political Economy" of Sex' began as an undergraduate anthropology paper, written with two roommates who spent the whole semester stoned in a valiant effort to make sense of Lévi-Strauss. The essay became a classic, widely acknowledged to have set the terms of feminist debate for the next couple of decades.

Like Mitchell, Rubin drew on Marx and Engels, Freud, Althusser, Lacan and Lévi-Strauss. As she explained it, Lévi-Strauss adds to the theory of primitive reciprocity the idea that marriages are the most basic forms of gift exchange, in which it is women who are the most precious of gifts. The incest taboo should then be understood as a mechanism that ensures such exchanges do indeed take place between families and groups. The gift of women has more profound consequences than other gift transactions: its results not just in reciprocity but kinship. In turn, kinship is a way of generating a social and political structure from manipulations of marriage and descent (Rubin with Butler 1994: 86). As she summarised the argument, 'kinship is the culturalization of biological sexuality on the societal level; psychoanalysis describes the transformation of the biological sexuality of individuals as they are enculturated' (Rubin 1975: 189).

The exchange of women, Rubin notes, is a seductive and powerful concept, since it places the oppression of women within a social system. But it is also deeply problematic. Not only is it difficult to argue that there would be no human culture at all without the exchange of women, the anthropological record shows that the exchange of women seems to occur in some cultures but far less in others. What is needed to account for this tapestry of historically and culturally diverse practices is a comprehensive 'political economy of sexual systems', not just one shorthand concept. But the problem went even deeper. Far from being based on the prior existence of two exclusive genders, the exchange of women and the taboo on incest and endogamy involves a prior suppression of extensive natural *similarities* between men and women, and an insistence on a rigid division of personality. Moreover, the incest taboo presupposes a prior, less articulate taboo on most or all forms of homosexuality.

Rubin adds that actual kinship systems have specific conventions regarding sex and gender. While these conventions vary enormously over time and between socio-sexual systems, individuals living in any one of them have to conform to a specific and closely circumscribed range of possibilities. Hence, each new generation, and each individual within it, must be engraved with particular conventions of sex and gender. Anthropology is equipped to chart the conventions but not their acquisition by individuals. Psychoanalysis, on the other hand, 'is a theory about the reproduction of kinship. [It] describes the residue left within individuals by their confrontation with the rules and regulations of sexuality of the societies to which they are born' (Rubin 1975: 183).

Rather than call all this patriarchy, Rubin coined the term 'sex-gender system' in order to allow for the existence of gender egalitarian societies as well as a wide range of gender-stratified systems. As she defined it, a sex/gender system was the historically constituted 'set of arrangements by which a society transforms biological sexuality into products of human activity, and in which these transformed sexual needs are satisfied' (Rubin 1975: 159). Certainly, many of these arrangements were oppressive to women, but not necessarily so, and not necessarily in the same way. Rubin concluded that 'patriarchy is a specific form of male dominance, and the use of the term ought to be confined to Old Testament-type pastoral nomads from where the term comes, or groups like them' (Rubin 1975: 167–168).

Rubin shared the conviction of many contemporary radicals that feminist reform was becoming much easier because the sex/gender system had lost many of its traditional functions. Since gender is socially constituted, feminists can aim for the elimination of the social system which creates sexism and gender. Furthermore, since all people are oppressed by having to *be* women or men in the first place, a feminist utopia should involve the elimination of obligatory sexualities and sex roles. It followed that the feminist movement should attempt to reorganise the domain of sex and gender in such a way that each individual's Oedipal experience would be less destructive. If adults of both sexes cared for children equally, primary object choice would be bisexual. If heterosexuality was not compulsory, this early love would not have to be suppressed, and the penis would not be overvalued. If kinship and the gender system were reorganised so men would not have overriding rights in women, the entire Oedipal drama would become a relic. Soon, such social trends would become the target of an increasingly militant, anti-feminist men's rights movement.

Engels, Marxism and 'materialist feminism'

In much of continental Europe and the UK and to a lesser extent in Canada, Australia and New Zealand, there was a robust tradition of socialist activism and Marxist scholarly debate. For many feminists in these countries, historical materialism was the natural language of reflecting on social injustice and organising for change, and Engels was seen as one of many writers in a broad and familiar intellectual tradition. From this perspective, Marxist analysis, with its overwhelming focus on the relations between workers and employers, needed to be enhanced or reconfigured so it would make sense of the situation of women and of spheres of life outside of the formal economy. In the US, especially during the period of McCarthyism in the 1950s and early 1960s, labour movements and Marxist theory were far less influential. The resurgence of social movements in the late 1960s changed all that. As the US sociologist Lise Vogel recalled, by the early 1970s:

> interest in the bearing of Marxist theory on women's liberation seemed perfectly normal – and not just to socialist feminists. Radical feminists also adopted and transformed what they understood to be Marxist concepts … Women's liberationists studied Marxist texts, wrestled with Marxist concepts, and produced a range of original formulations combining, or at least intermingling, Marxism and feminism. Their enthusiasm for this work is hard today to recapture.
>
> *(Vogel 2000: 152)*

A number of feminists used innovative versions of Marxist concepts to identify what they believed to be the deep material roots of an all-pervasive patriarchy. Some simply stated that women were an oppressed class, suggested that the relations between men and women were class relations, and that sexual politics were the politics of class domination.[2] For Nancy Chodorow (1978) and Dorothy Dinnerstein (1976), drawing on a particular version of psychoanalysis, it was asymmetrical parenting arrangements – and particularly women's overwhelming responsibility for mothering – which produced radically different dispositions in girls and boys, and so lay the universal basis for subconscious perpetuation of male dominance. Relying on a particular reading of the Marxist notion of alienation, the US legal scholar and radical feminist Catherine MacKinnon (1982) argued that it was the relations of heterosexuality, and sexual objectification in particular, which formed the material basis of women's oppression. In other words, 'sexuality is to feminism what work is to Marxism: that which is most one's own, yet most taken away'. It followed that consciousness-raising would allow women to articulate their shared experience of objectification, and so provide the groundwork for liberating political action. A related synthesis of feminist emphasis on fertility and reproduction and Marxist theory was published in 1981 by the Canadian scholar Mary O'Brien. *The Politics of Reproduction* drew on O'Brien's extensive experience as a midwife to argue that the seeds of patriarchy lay in men's attempts to compensate for their inability to bear babies. Women's liberation, then, should focus on demystifying of the process of reproduction, and in particular on the contradiction between the nature of women's reproductive labor and (male) ideological mystifications of it.

Perhaps the most literal application of materialism to relations between women and men was Shulamith Firestone's *The Dialectic of Sex: The Case for Feminist Revolution* (1970). A graduate in painting from the Art Institute of Chicago, Firestone argued that patriarchy had a physical rather than a cultural basis in women's childbearing work. Throughout history, in all stages and types of culture, she noted, women have been oppressed due to their biological function in reproducing the species. The fact that women and not men had babies led directly to the first division of labour based on sex, which was at the origin of all further social division into economic and cultural classes. Exploiting biological imperatives, men first imposed dependency and subordination on women, and then extended this domination to children, workers and people of colour. Patriarchy thus became the source of age, class and racial oppression. Like other radicals at the time, Firestone saw the family as a profoundly flawed institution. In contrast to them, however, she did not believe that abolishing it would stop women's oppression. In an argument that sparked endless controversies, she concluded that women must seize control over the means of *reproduction* in order to eliminate the sexual class system. Only a technological solution to the burdens of pregnancy and childbirth, such as test-tube babies, could end patriarchy.

Eventually, two themes in Engels' *Origin* and Marxist theory more generally became a particular focus of feminist debates. The first, debated with particular intensity in US feminist anthropology, concerned the claim that forms of male domination developed from gender-egalitarian prehistoric communities, deteriorated with the rise of private property and state institutions, and could end when social antagonisms and crises reached a particular stage. The second theme, taken up most extensively in countries with a strong tradition of socialist scholarship, concerned the way that production and reproduction, the division of labour and technological change were played out in unequal and exploitative relations between women and men.

When did it start?

While many feminists (and anti-feminists) believed that patriarchy stretched back as far as 'culture' itself, others strenuously argued that many ancient societies were matriarchal or at least 'woman centred' and goddess worshipping from the Palaeolithic era, 1.5–2 million years ago, until sometime around 3,000 BCE (Eller 2000). In the work of Engels and some of the authors he drew on, ancient peaceable, cooperative matriarchal societies were replaced by exploitative patriarchal ones with the 'world-historical defeat of the female sex'. Engels followed nineteenth-century social science in outlining a unilineal historical progression of social orders, but parted company with most contemporaries to argue that sexual asymmetry *worsened* with the emergence of private property, the adoption of more complex technologies, the rise of states, and the spread of capitalism. At the end of his life, Marx began sketching out multiple paths of human development, and began to consider whether communities of contemporary 'primitive' peoples might in fact provide a model for a future communist society, without the need to traverse multiple stages of the 'civilised' development whose many features he so vehemently criticised ('Drafts of a Letter to Vera Zasulich', in Shanin 1983; Krader 1974). In mainstream anthropology, narratives of linear human progression were discredited by the turn of the twentieth century. However, questions of ancient prehistory and anthropology of 'primitive' societies retained profound political significance in debates about the possibility of social change. If it could be proved that women were once powerful and respected, then biological arguments about their innate inferiority to men were false, and women would more easily reclaim dignity and authority. Conversely, the inability to come up with any examples of societies that were not male dominated could be used to prove the inevitability of patriarchy. As one of the participants later explained,

> [In the early 1970s] [t]here were dozens of little schemas about the ostensible overthrow of the supposed early Matriarchy and the invention of private property as the source of women's oppression … I doubt people who weren't there could begin to imagine the intensity with which people fought over whether or not there was an original Matriarchy, and whether its demise accounted for class differences and the oppression of women.
>
> *(Rubin with Butler 1994: 64)*

In 1980, in an influential reflection on a decade of feminist writing and debates, the US anthropologist Michelle Rosaldo (1980: 390) noted with some exasperation that current feminist uses of anthropology were deeply problematic. While it was good that the discipline was no longer ignored by leading social thinkers, feminist classics 'all introduce their texts with what seems to anthropologists a most old-fashioned evocation of the human record'. This was because they ignored the most basic anthropological principles and assumed that similar actions – such as talking to women friends, preparing meals, celebrating their fertility or making demands of sons – meant the same things regardless of time, place and context. As a result:

> these writers catalog the customs of the past in order to decide if womankind can claim, through time, to have acquired or lost such rightful 'goods' as power, self-esteem, autonomy, and status. Though these writers differ in conclusions, methods, and particulars of theoretical approach, all move from some version of Beauvoir's question, 'What is woman?' to a diagnosis of contemporary subordination and from that on to the queries: 'Were things always as they are today?' and then, 'When did "it" start?'

In the event, arguments about the existence of ancient matriarchy inspired some forms of peace and ecology activism, experiments in alternative lifestyles, feminist spirituality and woman-centred collectives, and debates about the possibility of non-patriarchal religions. They also overlapped with attempts of African diaspora scholars to chart a non-racist account of African past (see for example Amadiume 1997; Diop 1959). As Frantz Fanon, one of the most eloquent and influential critics of colonialism, put it, these writers nourished 'the secret hope of discovering beyond the misery of today, beyond the self-contempt, resignation and abjuration, some very beautiful and splendid era whose existence rehabilitates us both in regard to ourselves and in regard to others' (cited in Shepherd 2002: 169). Almost uniformly, however, accounts of ancient matriarchy failed to convince scholars trained in the relevant disciplines. Certainly, the sceptics noted, there have been – and are – many matrilineal and matrilocal societies, but these are not the same thing as matriarchies.[3] The anthropologist Joan Bamberger (1974) typically noted that while patriarchal societies seem to abound in fact as well as in theory, no historical or current matriarchies have been found, nor are there any primary sources recounting them. This fact, she stated drily, had not prevented lively public interest in primitive matriarchies, nor an outpouring of books and articles attesting to a former rule by women, and using the concept of a primitive matriarchy as a rationale for a new social order.

Importantly, scholarly consensus that ancient matriarchy was nowhere to be found was quite different from arguments that human societies had always been dominated by males. Using her own fieldwork as a starting point, the US Marxist anthropologist Eleanor Leacock, for example, argued that women were not always and everywhere subservient to men. To those who claimed that all surviving primitive societies oppressed women, she responded that the communities studied by anthropologists were a shadow of their previous form, and could not be taken as examples of what life was like before they came into contact with Europeans. Finally, Leacock entered into highly publicised debates with those who claimed that patriarchy was all-pervasive and timeless, and commented on the hostile environment that gave rise to such theories, and the interests they served. Importantly, despite her lifelong involvement in debates about women's subordination, Leacock followed Engels in her use of terminology. She did not advocate wholesale use of the concept of patriarchy, employed the term very sparingly herself, and argued that it was only appropriate for ancient Greece and Rome.

Contributors to the collection *Towards an Anthropology of Women* edited by Rayna Rapp Reiter and published in 1975 saw the early women's movement through somewhat different lenses, and had serious reservations about Leacock's argument that early human societies were sexually egalitarian.[4] However, they too drew extensively on Marxist theory, followed similar conventions on uses of the term patriarchy, rejected claims that women were always and everywhere subordinate to men, and put strong emphasis on the variability of relations between the sexes. Not only did the anthropological record show that cultures displayed a wide variation in the amount of sexual equality and inequality, but groups with the same mode of production often had radically different 'sexual status systems'; differently gendered social orders. *Towards an Anthropology of Women* was published by the socialist Monthly Review Press. It soon became a best-seller, and kept that press alive through years of financial difficulties. Importantly, while all the papers reflect on unequal and oppressive relations between women and men, they do not use the term patriarchy to describe them.

Early work of anthropologists such as Sherry Ortner, Michelle Rosaldo and Louise Lamphere took yet another approach: emphasising the enormous diversity of female experience and human cultures while insisting on the universal, transcultural and transhistorical nature of women's subordination.[5] As one of the authors later noted:

> The idea that male dominance was universal was [meant to be] somewhat shocking to many non-anthropologists, who seemed to think that although our own Western society is patriarchal, 'the anthropologists' would have some little stock of more reassuring cases of matriarchy and egalitarianism to bring forth.
>
> *(Ortner 1996: 173)*

Importantly, and despite their strong emphasis on 'universal sexual or gender asymmetry' and cultural devaluation of women, Ortner and other contributors to the *Woman, Culture and Society* volume too avoid the term patriarchy in discussing their findings. If anything, the authors discourage the use of the term, employ it sparingly to designate specific historical cultures such as in China and India, and are scathing about the historical existence of matriarchy.

Whatever side they took in these heated debates, by the late 1970s feminist anthropologists began revising their more categorical claims. In the process, they helped articulate themes which would become core preoccupations for the next generation of feminist scholarship. Narratives of linear human development, sweeping historical accounts, a unified category of 'women' and 'men', logically coherent indigenous cultures, the universality of the public and private dichotomy, the assumption that terms like asymmetry, subordination, equality, status and power meant the same thing in different times, places, and feminist texts – as well as the quest for origins of women's subordination – were all systematically challenged.[6]

Patriarchy is at home at home ...

> Regardless of class, and regardless of ownership (although these modify the situation in interesting ways), women have generally functioned as the property of men in the procreative and socializing aspect of the productive work of their society. Women constitute part of the means of production of the private family's mode of work. Patriarchy, in short, is at home at home. The private family is its proper domain.
>
> *(Kelly-Gadol 1976: 821)*

> the characteristic relation of human *reproduction* is patriarchy, that is, the control of women, especially of their sexuality and fertility, by men.
>
> *(Mackintosh 1977: 122)*

Whatever conclusion they came to, those who debated the origins of patriarchy also had housework to do, children to look after, and jobs to find. Here again, Marxist theory provided an important starting point. In 'Women: The Longest Revolution' (1966), Mitchell argued that feminist analyses of women's lives needed to grapple with four distinct aspects of life: production, reproduction, socialisation of children and sexuality. While her own work ended up dealing with the unconscious trans-generational transmission of patriarchal *culture*, most socialist feminists remained focussed on the more familiar spheres of contemporary production and reproduction. Employing established conceptual tools of political economy, they asked questions which had until then been ignored in Marxist scholarship. In doing so, they brought increasing sophistication to analyses of modern households, workplaces, industries and economies. Writing towards the end of the 'era of housewives', when (white) women's participation in the paid workforce was historically low, they initially focussed on two issues. The first concerned the unequal position of women in the labour market, and revolved around the Marxist concept of a 'reserve army of labour'. Women, it was argued, generally constituted a pool of people who were hired when there was a need for extra workers during labour shortages, and fired when things slowed down – or men returned home from wars. In turn, women's precarious position meant that they could be paid lower wages and given fewer entitlements than men, and so increase capitalists' profits. The second focus of socialist feminist theorising was on women's domestic labour. While participants in what came to be called the domestic labour debate generally did not use the concept of patriarchy, their conclusions became one of the cornerstones of its later feminist redefinitions.

As the English sociologist Veronica Beechey and the Canadian-born historian Barbara Taylor explained it in 1976, socialist feminists initially saw the main source of women's oppression in their ideological role in the family – as socialisers of children, and providers of sexual services, food and comfort to men (or in other words in servicing the families which reproduced patriarchal habits of mind). Exploitation in a capitalist society, they believed, only occurred in the workplace – and there the minority of women who worked for wages were exploited more than men because they were generally paid less for comparable work. The initial breakthrough came when some feminist writers pointed out that housewives' domestic labour also makes a tangible contribution to capitalist profits. If women did not feed and care for existing workers, and give birth to and nurture future ones, employers would not find anyone to hire. Besides, most of the things needed to sustain workers could not be used raw as bought from the shops, but had to be converted into meals and clean homes through women's housework. This suggested that women's sexual oppression by men in the family, and their economic exploitation as unpaid house workers for capitalism, were simply different sides of the same coin.[7] And since unpaid domestic labour made a direct contribution to employers' profits, some feminists argued that working-class women should organise on a class basis and demand wages for housework (Dalla Costa 1972). Others concluded that in order to achieve justice and equality with men, women must not only be given equal access to paid work, but provided with high quality socialised replacements for the necessary domestic and caring labour they performed.

The new understanding of family households as sites of production, and the redefinition of housework and childcare as labour processes, soon gave rise to a series of Marxian questions. Can we speak of the laws of motion of a patriarchal system? What kinds of sexual politics and struggle between the sexes can we see in societies other than advanced capitalist ones? What are the contradictions of the patriarchal system, and what is their relation to the contradictions of capitalism? Does patriarchy generate feminist struggle? (Hartmann 1979: 22). Could a mode of reproduction of people be posited, comparable to but separate from the mode of production? Was patriarchy, in effect, at home at home? And might answers to these questions help explain the origins of women's oppression? (Vogel 2000).

Considerations of these issues resulted in voluminous contributions and a great number of useful insights. However, as the debates became more complex and pedantic, many participants 'became restless with the abstract nature of the analyses being offered', and moved on to other concerns. As some key contributors later reflected, the domestic labour debate had a number of limitations. It was not just increasingly difficult to follow, it was haunted by several questionable common-sense assumptions, such as the notion that domestic labour is universal, that it is necessarily carried out by women, and that it is always unpaid rather than as part of the work of servants. In addition, by emphasising the *economic* nature of women's oppression, the debates downplayed the personal relations of sexuality and fertility, and the social construction of peoples' gendered psyches more generally. At the same time, much of the debate focussed on definitional issues, often without explaining why these mattered. Finally, the whole domestic labour debate was marred by the functionalist assumptions of most of the early theorists, who tended to imply that 'the family' existed because of its useful role in perpetuating a capitalist society.

Despite these limitations, the debates resulted in several enduring achievements. Writing in 1986, the Canadian sociologist Bonnie Fox noted that they transformed earlier feminist critiques of the oppressive nature of women's household work by showing its full extent and theorising its economic significance. The most important contribution of the domestic labour debate, she believed, was to come to an understanding of the relationship of the private household to capitalist commodity production. Fox (1986) concluded that one of the rewards of the debate, though one that most of its contributors did not antici-pate, was to make clear the limits of a class analysis for understanding issues about gender; most participants eventually became convinced that Marxist economic concepts must be more radically revised to take account of gendered dimensions of work, systematic inequalities between women and men, and men's appropriation of women's labour.

Towards a new synthesis

Theorisations of capitalism and patriarchy (or sex/gender systems) as two distinct systems of exploitation and inequality soon inspired reflections on the way that the two systems could be integrated without losing the strong points of radical feminism and of Marxism, or undermining the demand for an autonomous women's movement (see for example Kuhn and Wolpe 1978). As the US feminist economist Heidi Hartmann explained in a reconsideration of her earlier work, while capitalism and patriarchy remained distinct systems of social relations (which could sometimes be in conflict), in analyses of contemporary societies concerns with paid and unpaid work, and capitalist and male exploitation, must be integrated:

> Patriarchy is a system of social relations between men and women, governing the production and reproduction of people and their gender identities. Women are the primary producers in this arena (families, households, and neighbourhoods), but men maintain substantial control over this arena, and over women's labor, through the very structure of the reproductive unit (the family), the struc-ture of the production system (the capitalist workplace), and the control of the state apparatus to enforce patriarchal relations.
>
> *(Hartmann and Markusen 1980: 89)*

Importantly, Hartmann and Markusen stressed that men and women labour in both spheres. Nevertheless, 'just as the workplace is the primary, but not exclusive, locus of worker experience with capitalist social relations, so the household is the primary, but not exclusive locus of women's experience with patriarchal social relations'.

The public/private distinction itself, some argued, only emerged in its modern form in nineteenth-century Western countries. While it appeared natural to a generation brought up in the era of housewives, it was not appropriate to use it in making sense of societies in other times and places (Young 1980: 178).

As the limitations of distinct approaches became clearer, feminist theoreticians began calling for a broad new synthesis. It was more productive, they believed, to theorise a single, interwoven system of social relations where economies were always gendered, and different types of relations between women and men had a material basis. 'We need not merely a synthesis of feminism with traditional Marxism, but a thoroughly feminist historical materialism, which regards the social relations of a particular historical social formation as one system in which gender differentiation is a core attribute' (Young 1980: 181). Some went further, calling for a unified theory of class, gender and race, and providing a brilliant foundation of just such a scheme (Caulfield 1977; Sacks 1989). Yet others, prominent among them a group of French materialist feminists, programmatically attempted to integrate the two sides of the story through a radical revision of Marxist theory (Adkins and Leonard 2005). Perhaps the best-known of them was Christine Delphy, who argued that the core of material basis of women's oppression lies not in capitalist but in patriarchal relations of *production*. These revolve around the institution of marriage, defined in this instance as 'a labour contract in which the husband's appropriation of unpaid labour from his wife constitutes a domestic mode of production and a patriarchal mode of exploitation' (Delphy 1984).

By the end of the decade, most feminist writers agreed that forms of male domination and female subordination were not universal but varied substantially over time and between different societies and groups within them, and involved both ideological and material factors. 'We cannot write an accurate history of the West in relation to the Rest', Rapp typically wrote, 'until we stop assuming that our experiences subsume everyone else's ... We must simultaneously understand the differences and the similarities, but not by reducing them to one simple pattern' – or 'ransacking history to provide evidence of the existence of patriarchy in all times and places' (Rapp 1979: 511; 1977; Hartmann 1979: 10). The political economists Bridges and Hartmann similarly argued that while most known societies have been patriarchal, patriarchy was not a universal, unchanging phenomenon:

> Rather, patriarchy, the set of interrelations among men that allows men to dominate women, has changed in form and intensity over time ... Surely, class, race, nationality, and even marital status and sexual orientation, as well as the obvious age, come into play here.
>
> *(Hartmann 1979: 12)*

Some of the writers who emphasised the historicity of patriarchy went on to suggest more specific names to distinguish *differently patriarchal* societies and at times identified factors they believed were responsible for the transition from one form of patriarchy to another.

So what about patriarchy?

The overview of different uses, non-uses, critiques – and deliberate avoidance – of the term patriarchy outlined in this chapter shows that there was far more diversity in the 1970s than later commentaries allow for. To some feminists, patriarchy was a wilful, all-encompassing system which oppressed women:

> Patriarchy as a political structure seeks to control and subjugate women so that their possibilities for making choices about their sexuality, childrearing, mothering, loving, and labouring are cur- tailed. Patriarchy, as a system of oppression, recognizes the potential power of women and the actual power of men. Its purpose is to destroy woman's consciousness about her potential power, which derives from the necessity of society to reproduce itself. By trying to affect woman's consciousness, and her life options, patriarchy protects the appropriation of women's sexuality, their reproductive capacities, and their labour by individual men and society as a whole. The sexual organization to control women reflects the priorities of patriarchy.
>
> *(Eisenstein 1981: 14–15)*

Many influential writers reserved the term patriarchy for specific forms of social organisation which were literally ruled by fathers (rather than men in general), and employed a more general word, such as 'male-dominated', to designate the collectivity of 'gender asymmetrical' cultures. Even those many feminists who believed that the concept of patriarchy *did* provide the appropriate conceptual space in which a rigorous understanding of women's subordination could be elaborated did not agree on what the term meant, whether it referred to mentalities, systems of ideas, family dynamics, economies or all of these, and how it should be tackled. Theorisation of patriarchy most often focussed on habits of mind, sexuality, childbearing, and domestic relations more broadly. Feminists grappled with these core concerns through a spectrum of approaches spanning everyday behaviourist psychology, psychoanalysis, and several different versions of innovative and at times highly unorthodox materialism. And while most saw patriarchy as a more or less useful and precise *descriptive* term, some attempted to use it as an *analytical* concept, and develop a theory of patriarchy with a clear causality and predictive power, capable of explaining the rise of women's movements and providing a 'correct revolutionary strategy' (see also Vogel 2000). Those who crafted particularly complicated explanations using elaborate technical terms often sparked heated debates about elitism and the usefulness of theory for grassroots social movements in the first place (see for example *Papers on Patriarchy* 1978).

During the early 1970s (at least in English-language literature) feminists emphasising materialist analyses rarely referred to patriarchy. While radical feminists argued that patriarchal social relations as they defined them took political and analytical primacy over those of class, most feminists influenced by Marxist theory initially believed that capitalist relations of production, albeit analysed with feminist questions in mind, were the determining forces of social inequality. By the end of the decade, their analyses broadened. Capitalism and patriarchy, it was increasingly argued, were equally important, autonomous systems of oppression and inequality. It followed that radical and socialist feminist analyses both had merit, and need to be considered side by side through a dual system theory, or perhaps even one comprehensive and integrated theoretical scheme.[8]

* * *

Many first-generation feminist scholars wanted to examine one aspect of women's lives, looked around for a relevant theoretical framework and contextual information, found none that adequately suited their project, so set out heroically to construct a grand overview themselves. Professional anthropologists and social historians tended to appreciate the true enormity of the task. Rather than attempt a personal synthesis, they convened conferences, set up new journals, and called for interdisciplinary and collaborative projects so they could engage in 'collective theorising'. As Rayna Rapp put it in 1977, '[u]nravelling the origins of sexual hierarchies is a huge undertaking ... It will easily be decades before the feminist critique can do for us what a Marx, a Weber, a Freud, a Lévi-Strauss have done for their areas of inquiry'. Yet the point of feminist critique was fundamentally different from the process 'by which individual men, stunningly well-educated as scholars, and totally confident of their mission as critical thinkers, redefine a tradition, and give it a new direction'. Rather than trying to replicate this highly individualist project:

> What we are now attempting is something at once less grand and more consciously collective. For if we are children of the patriarchs of our respective intellectual traditions, we are also sisters in a women's movement which struggles to define new forms for social process in research and in action. In our role as sisters we aim for a shared, more reciprocal notion of engaged research.
>
> *(Rapp 1977: 15)*

As in other pioneering projects, many of the maps and conclusions drawn up by writers of the early second-wave women's movement proved to be inaccurate. Yet they helped to pose new questions and to articulate new ways of thinking; brought many of the underlying issues into sharper focus, and inspired ideas about the previously unthinkable. The intellectual models produced by the early feminists were intensely productive – of intellectual energy, personal and collective reforming zeal, new ways of seeing, social movement activism; they helped envision and in many instances think into existence new social categories.

The envisioning, activism and new questions contributed to existing intellectual ferment in the social sciences, and inspired a lot of detailed research. This in turn helped reconfigure conceptual tools, clarify and challenge theoretical approaches, and pose unexpected new questions. Some pioneered far-reaching challenges to the whole corpus of humanities and social sciences in the twenty-first century. The same intellectual ferment and feminist organising unsettled the lives, ideas and privileges of many men. Some reacted by finding new sources of economic security, family harmony and inner strength in ways which did not involve the domination of women. Others, described in the final chapter of this book, set out to reinvent patriarchy.

Notes

1 Later in life, Millett became seriously annoyed that her first, hastily written book continued to attract attention while her later work was largely ignored (Baumgardner 2002).
2 The 'Redstockings Manifesto' of 1969, cited in Kelly-Gadol (1976: 813).
3 Matrilineal societies are those where descent is traced through the mother and maternal ancestors; in matrilocal societies married couples live with or near the wife's parents, and so daughters live in (or near) the mother's house after marriage.
4 For a similar argument contained in the very first overview of anthropology in the first issue of *Signs*, see Stack *et al.* (1975).
5 Twenty years after that statement was published, several contributors to the Rosaldo and Lamphere book specifically recanted this assertion (Hoskins 2005: 1384).
6 For a sophisticated restatement of the arguments, see Coontz and Henderson (1986).
7 For an influential early formulation of this problematic, see Benston (1969).
8 For an eloquent case for such a unified vision, built round the concept of patriarchy, see Kelly (1979).

References

Adkins, Lisa and Diana Leonard (2005) 'Reconstructing French Feminism: Commodification, materialism and sex', in Diana Leonard and Lisa Adkins (eds) *Sex in Question: French materialist feminism*. Taylor & Francis e-Library.

Alexander, Sally and Barbara Taylor (1981) 'In Defence of "Patriarchy"', in Raphael Samuel (ed.) *People's History and Socialist Theory*. London: Routledge and Kegan Paul, pp. 370–374.

Amadiume, Ife (1997) 'Theorising Matriarchy in Africa: Kinship ideologies and systems in Africa and Europe', Ch. 3 in *Reinventing Africa: Matriarchy, religion and culture*. London and New York: Zed Books, pp. 71–88.

Bamberger, Joan (1974) 'The Myth of Matriarchy', in Michelle Zimbalist Rosaldo and Louise Lamphere (eds) *Woman, Culture, and Society*. Stanford, CA: Stanford University Press, pp. 261–280.

Baumgardner, Jennifer (2002) 'That Seventies Show', *Dissent Magazine* 49(3): 62–66.

Benston, Margaret (1969) 'The Political Economy of Women's Liberation', *Monthly Review* 21(4): 13–27.

Braude, Ann (2004) *Transforming the Faiths of Our Fathers: The women who changed American religion*. Basingstoke: Palgrave Macmillan.

Braude, Ann (2006) 'A Short Half-century: Fifty years of women at Harvard Divinity School', *Harvard Theological Review* 99(4): 369–380.

Caulfield, Mina Davis (1977) 'Universal Sex Oppression? A critique from Marxist anthropology', *Catalyst* 10–11: 60–77.

Chodorow, Nancy (1978) *The Reproduction of Mothering: Psychoanalysis and the sociology of gender*. Berkeley: University of California Press.

Coakley, Sarah (2013) *God, Sexuality and the Self: An essay 'on the Trinity'*. Cambridge: Cambridge University Press.

Coontz, Stephanie and Peta Henderson (1986) 'Property Forms, Political Power, and Female Labour in the Origins of Class and State Societies', in Stephanie Coontz and Peta Henderson (eds) *Women's Work, Men's Property: The origins of gender and class*. London: Verso, pp. 108–155.

Dalla Costa, Mariarosa (1972) 'Women and the Subversion of the Community', *Radical America* 6(1): 67–102.

Daly, Mary (1968) *The Church and the Second Sex*. New York: Harper & Row.

Daly, Mary (1973) *Beyond God the Father: Toward a philosophy of women's liberation*. Boston, MA: Beacon Press.

Daly, Mary (1978) *Gyn/Ecology: The metaethics of radical feminism*. Boston, MA: Beacon Press.

Daly, Mary (1998) *Quintessence … Realizing the Archaic Future: A radical elemental feminist manifesto*. Boston, MA: Beacon Press.

Davis, Natalie Zenon (1976) '"Women's History" in Transition: The European case', *Feminist Studies* 3(3/4): 83–103.

Delphy, Christine (1984) *Close to Home: A materialist analysis of women's oppression*. Amherst: University of Massachusetts Press.

Dinnerstein, Dorothy (1976) *The Mermaid and the Minotaur: Sexual arrangements and human malaise*. New York: Harper & Row.

Diop, Cheikh Anta (1959) *The Cultural Unity of Black Africa: The domains of matriarchy and patriarchy in classical Antiquity*. Chicago, IL: Third World Press.

Eisenstein, Zillah R. (1981) *The Radical Future of Liberal Feminism*. New York and London: Longman.

Eller, Cynthia (2000) *The Myth of Matriarchal Prehistory: Why an invented past won't give women a future*. Boston, MA: Beacon Press.

Engels, Friedrich (1972 [1884]) *The Origin of the Family, Private Property and the State, in light of the researches of Lewis H. Morgan*. Reprint, with an introduction and notes by Eleanor Burke Leacock. Translated by Alec West. New York: International Publishers.

Firestone, Shulamith (1970) *The Dialectic of Sex: The case for feminist revolution*. St Albans: Paladin.

Freud, Sigmund (1913) *Totem and Taboo*. Boston, MA: Beacon Press.

Freud, Sigmund (1939) *Moses and Monotheism*. New York: A. A. Knopf.

Fox, Bonnie (1986) 'Never Done: The struggle to understand domestic labour and women's oppression', in Roberta Hamilton and Michèle Barrett (eds) *Politics of Diversity: Feminism, Marxism and nationalism*. Montreal: Book Center, pp. 180–189.

Hartmann, Heidi (1979) 'The Unhappy Marriage of Marxism and Feminism: Towards a more progressive union', *Capital and Class* (Summer): 62–99.

Hartmann, Heidi and Ann R. Markusen (1980) 'Contemporary Marxist Theory and Practice: A feminist critique', *Review of Radical Political Economics* 12(2): 87–94.

Hoagland, Sarah Lucia and Marilyn Frye (2000) *Feminist Interpretations of Mary Daly*. University Park: Pennsylvania State University Press.

Hoskins, Janet (2005) 'Matriarchy', in *New Dictionary of the History of Ideas*, vol. 4, ed. M. C. Horowitz. Detroit, MI: Charles Scribner's Sons, pp. 1384–1389.

Kelly, Joan (1979) 'The Doubled Vision of Feminist Theory: A postscript to the "Women and Power" conference', *Feminist Studies* 5(1): 216–227.

Kelly-Gadol, Joan (1976) 'The Social Relation of the Sexes', *Signs* 1(4): 809–823.

Krader, Lawrence (ed.) (1974) *The Ethnological Notebooks of Karl Marx*, 2nd edn. Assen, The Netherlands: Van Gorcum.

Kuhn, Annette and Ann Marie Wolpe (eds) (1978) *Feminism and Materialism: Women and modes of production*. London: Routledge and Kegan Paul.

MacKinnon, Catherine (1982) 'Feminism, Marxism, Method, and the State', part 1, *Signs* 7(3): 515–544; part 2, *Signs* 8(4): 635–658.

Mackintosh, Mary (1977) 'Reproduction and Patriarchy: A critique of Meillassoux's *Femmes greniers et capitaux*', *Capital and Class* 2: 114–127.

'Mary Daly' (2004), in *Encyclopedia of World Biography*, 2nd edn, vol. 4, pp. 380–381. Gale Virtual Reference Library. Accessed 5 December 2016.

McCann, Sean and Michael Szalay (2005), 'Introduction: Paul Potter and the Cultural Turn', *The Yale Journal of Criticism* 18(2): 209–220.

Millett, Kate (1970) *Sexual Politics*. New York: Doubleday.

Mitchell, Juliet (1966) 'Women: The longest revolution', *New Left Review* 40: 11–37.

Mitchell, Juliet (1971) *Woman's Estate*. Harmondsworth: Penguin.

Mitchell, Juliet (1975) *Psychoanalysis and Feminism*. London: Penguin.

Mitchell, Juliet (2000) *Psychoanalysis and Feminism*. Reprinted with a new introduction. London: Penguin.

Morgan, Robin (1970) *Sisterhood Is Powerful*. New York: Random House.

O'Brien, Mary (1981) *The Politics of Reproduction*. Boston, MA: Routledge and Kegan Paul.

Ortner, Sherry B. (1996) 'So, Is Male to Female as Nature Is to Culture?' Ch. 7 in *Making Gender: The politics and erotics of Culture*. Boston, MA: Beacon Press.

Papers on Patriarchy (1978) London: Publications Distribution Cooperative and Women's Publishing Collective.

Rapp, Rayna Reiter (1977) 'The Search for Origins: Unravelling the threads of gender hierarchy', *Critique of Anthropology* 3(9–10): 5–24.

Rapp, Rayna (1979) 'Anthropology', *Signs* 4(3): 497–514.

Reiter, Rayna (ed.) (1975) *Towards an Anthropology of Women*. New York: Monthly Review Press.

Rich, Adrienne (1976) *Of Woman Born: Motherhood as experience and institution*. New York: Bantam.

Rosaldo, Michelle Zimbalist (1980) 'The Use and Abuse of Anthropology', *Signs* 5(3): 389–417.

Rubin, Gayle (1975) 'The Traffic in Women: Notes on the "political economy" of sex', in Rayna Rapp Reiter (ed.) *Towards an Anthropology of Women*. New York: Monthly Review Press, pp. 157–210.

Rubin, Gayle with Judith Butler (1994) 'Interview', *Differences: A Journal of Feminist Cultural Studies* 6 (2+3): 62–99.

Sacks, Karen (1989) 'Toward a Unified Theory of Class, Race, and Gender', *American Ethnologist* 16: 534–550.

Shanin, Teodor (1983) *Late Marx and the Russian Road: Marx and 'the peripheries of capitalism'*. New York: Monthly Review Press.

Shepherd, Nick (2002) 'The Politics of Archaeology in Africa', *Annual Review of Anthropology* 31: 189–209.

Stack, Carol B., M. D. Caulfield, V. Estes, S. Landes, K. Larson, P. Johnson, J. Rake and J. Shirck (1975) 'Anthropology', *Signs* 1(1): 147–159.

Vogel, Lise (2000) 'Domestic Labor Revisited', *Science and Society* 64(2): 151–170.

Young, Iris Marian (1980) 'Socialist Feminism and the Limits of the Dual System Theory', *Socialist Review* 10(2–3): 169–188.

6

PATRIARCHY IN FEMINIST SCHOLARSHIP AND ACTIVISM FROM THE 1980S TO THE END OF THE MILLENNIUM

Well, I can remember the first time I ever heard patriarchy used – it terrified me. (Laughter) It sounded so ideological, heavy, and – I don't know – all the things that at that age I wasn't … I think it was 1980. I remember Jean [Grossholz] going around and saying to people during coffee breaks, 'We have to talk about patriarchy'. And I thought, 'Oh no, not patriarchy – I don't know what patriarchy is, and furthermore, it's not the kind of language I use!'

(Cohn and Enloe 2003: 1187)

I am one of those scholars who has stopped using the term 'patriarchy' in my writing and teaching … the term conjures up the kind of simplistic thinking that sometimes characterized early work in women's studies and also has the potential to suggest a transhistorical sameness that undermines the very idea of history … It is not that I no longer believe that in a variety of ways in different places and across time women are systematically disadvantaged compared to men of the same social group, but because the term can substitute for analysis. Oppressed by what or whom? Why?

(Rupp 2008: 136–137)

In Western countries, the 1980s saw the crisis-ridden end of the long post-war economic boom. The era of housewives, with stable marriages of male breadwinners and female homemakers (at least for the majority of white families) began to be slowly transformed. The golden years of capitalism were replaced by slower economic growth, deepening globalisation and rising social inequality. The imagery of a machine-like Fordist system gave way to narratives of disorganised capitalism. State institutions which seemed all-powerful came under sustained attack by a resurgent political Right. Many feminist and New Left activists found themselves defending the education, health and welfare provisions they had previously criticised against savage funding cuts. De-industrialisation, and with it the loss of blue-collar jobs, reduced the 'white dividend' most white workers expected, and exacerbated racial tensions. In Eastern Europe, unpopular socialist regimes began to falter. Countries of the global South were drawn more closely into new relations of dependence with the metropole. The capacity of governments to make decisions opposed by global institutions and multinational corporations diminished; the gap between the rich and poor grew. While trade, finance and production internationalised at a growing pace, national labour movements were weakened. Feminist struggles for reproductive rights, no-fault divorce, childcare, equal pay and equitable access to higher education and the professions became the target of an anti-feminist backlash. Many young women supported equal rights but repudiated feminism, linked as it was in hostile media and popular imagination with badly dressed, humourless, men-hating lesbians (Scharff 2012).

Social theories too were shaken up. Many earlier radical certainties – and structuralist analyses – lost much of their persuasive power. Influential groups of writers began to focus exclusively on complex cultural processes. Others began to emphasise social movements and people's agency, yet others brought new sophistication to analyses emphasising the historicity and contingency of apparently timeless and fixed social arrangements. In historical scholarship, there was a broad shift from the study of livelihoods, populations, economies and social movements to the exploration of representations, language, perception and discourse. Commenting on the 'cultural turn' that social sciences took in the 1980s, the US sociologist and historian Bill Sewell noted that:

during the very period when historians have gleefully cast aside the notion of structural determination, the shape of our own social world has been fundamentally transformed by changes in the structures of world capitalism … somehow, at the very time when particularly powerful changes in social and economic structures are manifested evermore insistently in our daily lives, we cultural historians have ceased not only to grapple with such structures but even to admit their ontological reality.

(Sewell 2005: 520)

People of colour in metropolitan countries, and those in the global South, articulated a further challenge to Western social and political thought. Metropolitan theory, critics argued, needed to be 'provincialised' to take account of its specific local making and flavour; 'southern theory', or the writings of non-Western scholars, should be studied alongside the work of metropolitan ones (Chakrabarty 2000). In collections of ethnographic evidence, international development and social movement literature, perceptive commentators noted, people from 'primitive' indigenous cultures appear as informants – or else as objects of humanitarian interventions – but almost never as theorists in their own right.

Appreciating the importance of such arguments, some scholars began to adopt a new approach to the interplay between structure, agency and place. What people think, own and can do, they argue, is strongly constrained by the local and global structures they live in. But those structures are constantly being reconstructed and interpreted by human action, not just in terms of material environment, laws and institutions, but also ideas, dreams and desires (Ortner 1996). As the Australian sociologist Raewyn Connell (2011: 4) put it:

Social practices – including labour, care and struggle – are endlessly bringing new realities into existence. This is easily said, difficult to keep in mind. It is easier to think of the world as composed of things that we bump against like rocks – a family, a bank, a population, capitalism, patriarchy. But the storm of time keeps blowing: not only destroying what previously appeared solid, but creating and destroying and creating again.

Critiques of imperial feminism

Women's movements were part of the storm which had shaken up the social sciences. At home and abroad, ethnocentric and racist assumptions were challenged by women of colour. In the US, activists noted, feminism will never be taken up by black women if it put one's womanhood over and above one's race. Platitudes about racial solidarity could not rectify problems created by ethnocentric analyses. Particularly offensive was feminists' routine analogy between the oppression of white women and blacks – as well as the all too frequent complaints of white university students that discussions of racism and the experiences of minority women were irrelevant to feminism (Alexander 2004; Simons 1979; Hull *et al.* 1982; James *et al.* 2009; Hobson 2016). Equally insulting was the ignorant assumption that African American and other minority women in the metropole and women in countries of the global South had no prior experience as activists and theoreticians (see for example Guy-Sheftall 2008). In Britain, women of colour explained, many sisters did not join the women's movement because they saw it as racist in both theory and practice, or because they had other, more urgent, priorities and allegiances (Amos and Parmar 1984; Trivedi 1984). Black women in Britain, Amina Mama noted, may come from any part of an African continent so diverse that a single nation may have 250 languages. To generalise for the whole of Africa, she concluded, borders on the foolish, and in respect of the three continents from which black women in Britain originate must be the height of folly (Mama 1984). In Australia, indigenous women wrote of generations of dispossession by white people, asserted that they identified as Aboriginal first and women second, and pointed out that their priorities, such as land rights, racism and protection of sacred sites, were different to those of the predominantly white women's movement (Huggins 1994; Lake 2003).

'Under Western eyes', non-capitalist economies appeared backward, and the cultural practices of their peoples feudal residues blocking the path to modernisation and economic development. The lives and considered decisions of Third World women appeared stuck in primitive patriarchal 'tradition'; their preoccupations invisible or misunderstood and labelled superstitious and backward (Mohanty 1988; 2003). Why, for example, are women in contemporary Afghanistan seen as oppressed by ancient 'Afghan values' when the country has undergone decades of massive and traumatic changes, different groups deal with these changes in quite different ways, and ordinary women are rarely asked about their own strategic priorities? Why are dowry-murders in contemporary India interpreted in the context of ancient religious teachings rather than domestic violence (Narayan 1997)? Why are women who veil seen as dupes or victims of patriarchy, rather than as people making considered and complicated choices about their lives?

Not appreciating complex local circumstances and power dynamics, 'imperial feminism' came up with offensive stereotypes such as the passive, submissive and self-sacrificing Asian woman oppressed by her patriarchal family; the African victim of ignorance and timeless patriarchal tradition; and the strong and brave African American woman victimised by the black men in her community (Amos and Parmar 1984; Trivedi 1984; Mama 1984). The world, the critics charged, was far more complicated. White women were often complicit in racism and benefitted from imperialism abroad and racial discrimination at home. Campaigns to make streets safe for women frequently resulted in vigilante violence against black men. Rather than being weak and compliant, women in South and East Asia and the Muslim Middle East bargained with patriarchy according to the quite different resources available to them at different stages of their lives – even if their resistance sometimes did not lead anywhere, and did not make sense in terms of on an economic model of utility-maximising individuals (Kandiyoti 1988; 1998). The exotic historical examples which illustrated some of the best-known feminist arguments for the existence of a transhistorical patriarchy – such as veiling, genital cutting and widow burning, became the focus of particularly heated debates (Mani 1998; Mayo 2000; Ahmed 1992; Walley 1997). As one commentator noted, the current obsession in the West with addressing what are believed to be abhorrent cultural practices seems routinely to detract from far more pressing and lethal forms of everyday oppression such as lack of land, food and clean water, not to mention war, drought and international isolation. It is always easier he concludes, 'to oppose their rites than our wrongs' (Silverman 2004: 432).

Cross-cultural encounters at large international conferences, some organised under United Nations auspices, provided another forum for shaking up Western feminist thought. At stake were not just ethno-centric concepts and analyses, but conflicts between delegations that saw capitalist economic relations as a source of women's oppression, and those from countries such as the US who believed that capitalism was the most efficient way to organise economies (Ghodsee 2010). This debate has been an uncomfortable, even painful, process. Eventually, it resulted in analyses combining a strong recognition of difference with an emphasis on solidarity and common struggle, as well as examinations of globalisation as a gendered process, and new forms of transnational feminist organising (Connell 2011: 116–117). The concept of inter-sectionality, developed independently by a number of writers, became an influential way of simultaneously attending to issues of race, gender and class (see McCall 2005; May 2015; Collins and Bilge 2016).

Already in the 1970s, some writers cautioned against uncritical use of second-hand concepts. By the 1980s, lone voices turned into a chorus. A paper questioning the usefulness of gender as a category of historical analysis, written by the US historian Joan Scott, was cited in innumerable feminist works. As Scott put it, 'we must become more self-conscious about distinguishing between our analytic vocabulary and the material we want to analyze. We must find ways (however imperfect) to con-tinually subject our categories to criticism, our analyses to self-criticism' (Scott 1986: 1065; Butler and Scott 1992). Many of the influential feminist writers who, in the 1970s, helped define patriarchy, published self-critical reflections on their earlier work (see for example Rich 1986; Chodorow 1989; Mitchell 2000). Rubin typically noted that, with the advantage of hindsight, her 'Traffic in Women' paper contained more sweeping and grandiose claims, or 'innocent uni-versalism', than she would be later comfortable with: 'at the time I wrote "Traffic," there was a still a kind of naive tendency to make general statements about the human condition that most people, including me, would now try to avoid' (Rubin 2011: 88).

The debates brought up some really tricky and interesting questions. How do you study societies where gender is not a central organising principle, or just one among others such as war/peace, young/old, plant/animal? (Atkinson 1982: 247; Boydston 2008)? How do you deal with the very real possibility that both the importance (or not) of gender as a key organising principle of society, and the way it is understood, changes over time? Write about people who move between several different gender-like categories over their lifecourse? Or translate the word gender into the many languages which do not have any suitable equivalent terms? How do you think through compelling arguments that kinship is a historically changing, invented category for tidying up relations between people who end up living together, rather than a set of fixed, universal 'kinship rules which prescribe patterns of sexual dominance and subordination (Carsten 2000; 2003)?'[1] Can the script of the Oedipal drama be rewritten in particular historical circumstances? How do you deal with the fact that the distinction between public and private spheres works quite differently in different times and places (Landes 1998; Thornton 1995; Helly and Reverby 1992; Scott and Keates 2004)? That the making of a universal category of woman has a number of quite specific local histories? How do you employ all these complicated points in contesting the assumption that women from poorer countries and communities, or those practising Hinduism or Islam, are automatically subject to greater patriarchy? Has colonialism, as Gayatri Spivak famously put it, been justified by 'white men saving brown women from brown men'? And given all these difficulties, who has the authority to speak? (Spivak 1985: 7–8, 120–130).

The feminist scholarship which tackled these complex issues was vastly different from that of the previous decade. In the 1970s, feminists struggled to find books or university courses dealing with women and gender:

> this was the period when mimeographed articles began to circulate around the country through a kind of informal underground network ... before the Internet and before the widespread availability of photocopying, smeared and blurry purple-ink pages were what most of us depended upon.
>
> *(Rothenberg 2008: 73)*

By the end of the millennium, what was once the subversive, intellectual arm of a thriving grassroots movement became professionalised, with feminist conferences, journals, associations, publishers, book series, prizes, fellowships, archives, institutes, list servs and foundations. In the

United States alone, there were around 700 women's studies programs and more than 30 feminist academic journals. As the authors of one overview text put it:

> The acceptance of feminist research within academia has been painfully denied for far too long. Once (largely) adopted, the floodgates have been burst asunder with an absolute deluge of writings. Since the early 1980s the pace of debate has been intense, the range of research immense.
>
> *(Kemp and Squires 1997: 7)*

Feminist theory, when pursued rigorously enough, could now secure jobs and promotions. In many Western countries, feminists were appointed to senior academic, administrative and government posts; those who continued their involvement in time-consuming political campaigns found it ever more difficult to combine activism and university work (Stacey 2000: 1190; Messer-Davidow 2002).

The increasingly complex and sophisticated tapestry of feminist scholarship, with its regional and disciplinary differences, became less and less accessible to those without extensive university training (Barrett 1992: 116). During the same period, a dispersed feminist thirst for justice, as well as feminist inroads into higher education, white collar occupations and the professions, engendered a mass market for feminist classics and popular overviews of feminist thought. And just as in the 1970s anthropologists objected to feminist uses of old-fashioned versions of human record, academics now complained that sisters out in the human services were using old-fashioned versions of feminist theory. 'A strange disconnect exists between the massive body of scholarly research on gender, militarism, and peace-building', one international development academic complained, 'and on-the-ground practices in postconflict societies, where essentialized ideas of men as perpetrators of violence and women as victims continue to guide much program design' (Moran 2010: 261).

As the quotes at the beginning of this chapter illustrate, this process had its counterpart in thinking with patriarchy. Many feminist academics stopped using the concept in their work. Some, inspired by the French theorist and historian Michel Foucault, went further, and rejected commonly used categories, patriarchy among them, as oppressive impositions on the lives of individual people. In the 1970s and 1980s, the radical feminist historian Judith Bennett complained, historians of women readily talked about patriarchy; by the early 2000s, it was barely whispered. When she looked at articles published from 2001 through 2004 in the three major English-language women's history periodicals, she found that not one of the nearly 300 articles had the word patriarchy, or any of its variants, in the title (Bennett 2006: 21–22). The US historian Leila Rupp exemplified this approach, noting that she does not use patriarchy any more, and corrects students when they do so, because they use it instead of an explanation. When scholars use different and what they see as more precise terms, she added, it therefore does not make their work any less feminist and politically committed. Quite the contrary, *not* thinking with patriarchy should result in sharper analysis and more effective social action (Rupp 2008: 136).

Feminist Frameworks, written by the US feminist scholars Alison Jaggar and Paula Rothenberg, is a good example of an influential feminist text which followed this course. First published in 1978, it quickly became one of the most widely used texts in women's studies. The authors' brief and respectful introductions to different feminist frameworks were incorporated into other overview texts, and cited innumerable times by university students. The authors note that the frameworks are far more complex than brief characterisations can encompass, and theory-making is akin to a dialogue, constantly remedying deficiencies in earlier accounts. They use terms such as women's subordination, 'institution of gender', 'women's oppression' or 'overwhelmingly sexist society', but not patriarchy to characterise the current situation. Even the brief exposition of radical feminism does not employ the term patriarchy. The only references to patriarchy in a nine-page index are to texts of three excerpts. The second edition of the text came out in 1984, and the third, which included two additional feminist frameworks: 'Through the Lens of Race, Gender, Class and Sexuality: Multiculturalism', and 'Women's Subordination World Wide: Global Feminism', in 1993.

In the first two editions of *Feminist Frameworks*, Jaggar and Rothenberg argue forcefully that feminists need a systematic and 'comprehensive theory of the position of women in society'. By 1993, the authors note that:

Twenty-five years of disciplinary and interdisciplinary research have demonstrated that much early feminist theory was not only enormously visionary and fruitful but also embarrassingly simplistic. This quarter-century of scholarly work, coupled with contemporary postmodern challenges to the possibility of complete and comprehensive ('totalizing') social analyses ... has made many feminists sceptical that any single framework will be adequate for all situations. We share this scepticism.

(Jaggar and Rothenberg 1993: xvi)

To make clear that such scepticism was not the same as rejection of all theorising, the third edition included a new section called 'Why theory?' With several exceptions, all as low-key synonyms for a male-dominated society, the editorial sections in the third edition do not make use of the term patriarchy.

Belated grand overviews

Not all feminist writers avoided thinking with patriarchy, however. The influential US feminist writers Marilyn French and Gerda Lerner completed grand overviews of transhistorical patriarchy they had embarked on years earlier. Gerda Lerner's *Creation of Patriarchy* (1986) and *Creation of Feminist Consciousness* (1993) surveyed 6,000 years of human history in order to outline and theorise the origins and perpetuation of women's subordination. A prolific US historian and charismatic public speaker, Lerner stressed that depriving women of the knowledge of their own history was at the root of their subordination. Making this systematic history visible, she believed, was a 'radical and transformative' contribution to women's liberation. Written years after the search for origins was discredited in mainstream feminist scholarship, and with the benefit of critical input from a number of colleagues, Lerner introduced *Creation of Patriarchy* with a number of disclaimers. She was not really searching for origins, but rather for 'the history of the patriarchal system'. There must have been many different ways in which the transition to patriarchy took place, forms of patriarchy differed in different societies, class and race were as important as gender in accounting for women's subordination, and ideas and texts as well as material relations were important in explaining the capacity of patriarchy to resist change over time.

Disclaimers over, Lerner set out to chart 'the relationship of women to the making of the world's symbol-system, their exclusion from it, their efforts at breaking out of the systematic educational disadvantaging to which they had been subjected, and finally, their coming into feminist consciousness'. She attempted to 'trace, by means of historical evidence, the development of the leading ideas, symbols, and metaphors by which patriarchal gender relations were incorporated into Western civilisation'. After surveying the Assyrian, Babylonian, Amorite, Sumerian and Hebrew civilisations of the ancient Near East and ancient Greece, Lerner placed the origins of patriarchal rule into the second millennium BCE. Writing in the grand tradition of Johann Bachofen, she argued that the symbols and metaphors for gender 'represent historical artifacts, from which it is possible to deduce the social reality which gave rise to [them]. By tracing the changes in metaphor or image, it should be possible to trace the underlying developments in society'. Lerner concluded that 'women and men have entered the historical process under different conditions and have passed through it at different rates of speed' (Lerner 1986: 11, 226).

Marilyn French's novel, *The Women's Room* (1977), was translated into twenty languages, sold more than 20 million copies, and made her one of the best-known feminist figures. Her three-volume *From Eve to Dawn: A History of Women in the World*, published in 2002 but completed a decade earlier, presented a vast world history of the patriarchal system responsible for the injustices depicted in her novel. The story begins thousands of years before the world's first revolution in which men obtained power over women. Over time, patriarchy institutionalised male dominance, and guaranteed it by a set of interlocking structures that perpetuate the power and authority of an elite class of men over all other humans and grant all men power and authority over women of their class. Assisted by a large number of feminist scholars, most of whom did not share the basic idea behind the project, the different chapters assembled a massive catalogue of patriarchal oppression of women, and ended on a hopeful note with the emergence of feminism.

Words, patriarchy and the speaking subject

Lerner and French had far more influence on vernacular feminist theorising than on feminist scholarship. The opposite was true of the work
of several French psychoanalytic theorists who employed the concept of
patriarchy in exploring the pervasive influence of patriarchal language
and systems of thought on the making of women's subjectivity. Many
of the key works of writers such as Luce Irigaray, Julia Kristeva and
Hélène Cixous were written in the 1970s, but were translated and
taken up by Anglo-American feminist scholars in the 1980s and 1990s.
One of those who helped articulate 'French feminism' to an English-
speaking audience is the Norwegian literary scholar Toril Moi. In her
controversial comparison between what she regarded as Anglo-American
and French feminist writing, Moi concluded that authors such as Kristeva
and Irigaray provide a more powerful and effective critique of patriarchal
culture than their Anglo counterparts. The concept of patriarchy was a
key part of her argument. As she explained it:

> patriarchal oppression consists of imposing certain social standards
> of femininity on all biological women, in order precisely to make
> us believe that the chosen standards for 'femininity' are natural ...
> Patriarchy has developed a whole series of 'feminine' characteristics
> (sweetness, modesty, subservience, humility, etc.) ... Kristeva's
> emphasis on *femininity as a patriarchal construct* enables feminists to
> counter all forms of biologistic attacks from the defenders of
> phallocentrism.
>
> *(Moi 1989)*

Like many of the feminist theoreticians described in Chapter 5, both
Kristeva and Irigaray believed that sex-role socialisation theories could
not adequately explain the production of *sexed* subjects within patriarchy. Freudian and Lacanian psychoanalysis was a far better starting
point, but only if radically revised to deal adequately with patriarchy,
and both women and men.

One of Irigaray's most influential works is *Speculum of the Other
Woman*, published in French in 1973 and first translated into English in
1985. Originally a PhD thesis in linguistics (she already had one in

philosophy), Irigaray drew on and critiqued Freud and Lacan, as well as Western philosophers such as Plato, Aristotle, Descartes, Kant, Hegel and Heidegger, to explain why 'our culture' systematically ignores and devalues women. Like Millett and Mitchell, Irigaray argues that women must fight for equal wages, and against discrimination in employment and education. However, remedying women's social and economic position is not enough, since it would leave the cultural source of women's oppression – a patriarchal depiction of feminine identity – untouched. The patriarchal philosophical tradition, Irigaray claims, defines the female only in contrast to the male – as its absence, complement, inversion, or inadequate approximation. 'Patriarchy does not prevent women from speaking', she notes; it refuses to listen when women do not speak 'universal', that is, as men. To remedy this, she sets out to model non-masculine language, a new form of expression that subverts the existing language system and enables women to speak as women (Stone 2006: 126, 133). The Western culture which denies sexual difference and construes it hierarchically, Irigaray contends, has its roots in the instinctive, bodily urge of men to assert themselves against women. Baby boys, she argues, have a particular problem negotiating separation from their mothers. Men respond to this difficulty by constructing mothers, and by extension, all women, as 'nature from which he has to differ' hierarchically, and which men must transcend and control (Stone 2006: 129). For Irigaray, patriarchy is the social manifestation of masculine libidinal economy and will remain the order of the day until the repressed 'feminine feminine' is set free (Tong 1998: 203).

In the early nineteenth century, the German philosopher Hegel used ancient Greek texts and the institutions they described to think through profound philosophical problems. Treating Hegel's work as an accurate depiction of Greek society, Irigaray in turn used Hegel's account in her own reflections on the family and political life. In order to depose patriarchy, she concluded, laws need to be changed to recognise 'sexuate rights'. As part of her active contribution to the women's movement in Italy, from the early 1990s Irigaray collaborated with the Commission for Equal Opportunities for the region of Emilia-Romagna on developing citizenship training, both for adults and children, through respect for gender difference as a key to respecting other differences.

Criticised as an essentialist, Irigaray and her supporters defend her engagement with essentialism as a strategy. While many contemporary interpreters now accept this view, strategic essentialism remains a controversial aspect of Irigaray's work (Donovan 2016). Essentialist or not, Irigaray continues to think with patriarchy. In a collection of conversations published in 2006, patriarchy is used as a basic description of 'our culture' and 'our tradition'; something so comprehensive, thickly woven and logically coherent that it is possible to speak of it as a wilful subject: such as 'patriarchy did not respect' female divinities; an 'oedipal logic of patriarchy'; and concepts 'manipulated by patriarchy' (Irigaray and Pluháček 2008).

The representation of 'French feminism' in English-language commentary has been contested. Most activists in the women's movement in France identify with one or another version of materialist feminism and are seriously annoyed that they are left out of English-language accounts of French feminism (Delphy 1995; Adkins and Leonard 2005). In addition, while Kristeva and Irigaray are usually discussed together in English language texts, the positions of these apparent twins are 'extreme poles apart' when judged from a feminist point of view. The Australian philosopher Elizabeth Grosz, for example, points out that while Kristeva remains committed to psychoanalysis as an explanatory framework, Irigaray employs it in all sorts of idiosyncratic and subversive ways. Kristeva is so consistently critical of 'feminists', to whom she attributes naive and simplistic analyses, that many commentators see her as anti-feminist. Irigaray is playful, poetic, experimental, rambling, difficult to read and joyously inconsistent; Kristeva erudite, dry, serious and scholarly (Grosz 1989: 101–104). Unlike Kristeva and Irigaray, Grosz uses the word patriarchy sparingly, and commends most highly the work of their contemporary Michèle Le Doeuff, whose exploration of the detailed historical production and interpretation of different kinds of philosophical knowledge, and their selective adoption by the French education system 'open philosophy to its own historicity' (Grosz 1989: 228).

Patriarchy plays a more central role in other commentaries on 'French feminism'. A chapter dealing with feminist literary criticism in a widely used guide to cultural studies written by the US academic Lois Tyson, for example, outlines 'traditional gender roles', summarises feminist principles, and discusses getting beyond patriarchy and the work of the three French feminists (Tyson 2014). Despite trivial objections, Tyson argues, feminist critique is well founded when one stops to listen, carefully and respectfully, to what it actually says. Thinking with patriarchy as a wilful entity is at the heart of this message. Tyson defines patriarchy as 'any culture that privileges men by promoting traditional gender roles'. Patriarchy promotes the belief that women are innately inferior to men. It continually exerts forces that undermine women's self-confidence and assertiveness. Whenever patriarchy wants to undermine a behaviour, it portrays that behaviour as feminine. Patriarchy treats women, whatever their role, as objects. Although feminists differ about many things, and so it is appropriate to talk about feminisms (in plural), Tyson argues that they all agree on some key points. First, 'women are oppressed by patriarchy economically, politically, socially, and psychologically; patriarchal ideology is the primary means by which they are kept so'. Second, 'in every domain in which patriarchy reigns, woman is the *other*: she is objectified and marginalised, defined only by her difference from male norms and values, defined by what she (allegedly) lacks and what men (allegedly) have'. However, patriarchy operates differently in different countries; even in the same country, cultural differences affect women's experience of patriarchy. For example, a black woman in the US is oppressed by patriarchy not just because she is a woman, but because she is a black woman, a category historically defined in the US as less valuable than the category of white woman.

Patriarchy and the subjugation of nature

The emphasis on patriarchy as a source of harmful ideas and systems of thought is shared by a number of leading feminist environmentalist philosophers and activists, particularly those close to radical feminist thought. Their distinctive contribution to thinking with patriarchy is to link the domination of women and nature. As Causey's entry on ecofeminism in the *Environmental Encyclopaedia* explains, while ecofeminist writers come from different disciplines and strands of feminism, they share a common belief that there are important historical, experiential, symbolic and theoretical connections between the domination of women and the domination of nature. This gender bias, ecofeminists claim, has dominated Western culture and led to a patriarchal, masculine, value-oriented hierarchy. Central to this patriarchal framework is a pattern of thinking that generates normative dualisms. These are created when paired complementary concepts such as male/female, mind/body, culture/nature and reason/emotion are seen as mutually exclusive and oppositional. As a result of socially entrenched gender bias, the more 'masculine' member of each dualistic pair is identified as the superior one (Causey 2003: 412; see also Warren 1993). However, ecofeminists such as the US philosopher Karen Warren (1994) make a clear distinction between their approach, which is compatible with a multiplicity of feminist theories, and a simplistic 'ecofeminine' one, which equates women and femininity with caring for nature. The Australian ecofeminist philosopher Val Plumwood goes further. She associates the concept of patriarchy with radical feminism, criticises it as reductionist and unhelpful, and does not use it in her influential book, *Feminism and the Mastery of Nature* (Plumwood 1993; 1994: 83).

* * *

Despite scholarly cautions, many feminist professional textbooks continue to draw on grand overviews and a powerfully drawn notion of patriarchy. In a chapter on 'Feminisms and Intrapartum Care' in a US text on *Essential Midwifery Practice*, for example, Mary Stewart (2010) depicts patriarchy as an ideology which makes contemporary society profoundly unequal. Stewart passionately believes that feminist thought needs to form the basis of holistic midwifery care. This should start with carefully listening to women and supporting them in making decisions, as equals and partners in control of their own bodies. Stewart explains that there are now many different strands of feminism which, despite many disagreements, have a lot in common. They share a concern for and a desire to improve women's lot in society, and generally agree that Western society is intrinsically patriarchal, hierarchical and unequal. Stewart defines patriarchy as 'an ideology that justifies and perpetuates male dominance and, within patriarchal social systems, power, benefits and burdens are unevenly distributed such that men, their values and characteristics are valued more highly than women'. The texts she refers to by Kirkley (2000) and Rafael (1996) define patriarchy in a similar way, and in their turn refer to French (2002) and Lerner (1986). As Rafael (1996: 4) explains:

> Patriarchy may be thought of as an ideology that justifies and perpetuates male dominance through valuing men, their characteristics, and their activities while at the same time devaluing women and their characteristics and activities. Patriarchy has not always been the prevailing ideology but rather developed over a period of several millennia to be firmly in place by about 6000 BCE.

A rupture in patriarchal systems of thought

In contrast to philosophical and ecofeminist work emphasising *continuity* of patriarchal *systems of thought*, the 1980s and 1990s also saw a number of publications focussed on profound *discontinuities* in patriarchal ideas and social relations. The Australian political philosopher Carole Pateman made a particularly influential and ambitious contribution to such work. In *The Sexual Contract* (1988), she at once defended the use of the concept of patriarchy and recast its meaning. As she put it:

> Some have argued that the problems with the concept are so great that it should be abandoned. To follow such a course would mean that, to the best of my knowledge, feminist political theory would then be without the only concept that refers specifically to the subjection of women that singles out the form of political right that all men experience by virtue of being men. If the problem has no name, patriarchy can all too easily slide back into obscurity beneath the conventional categories of political analysis.
>
> *(Pateman 1988a: 20)*

To sharpen the concept into an effective tool of political analysis, Pateman depicts patriarchy as a system subject to radical transformation and discontinuity arising out of new, discursively constituted modes of contractual political and economic governance.

In *Psychoanalysis and Feminism* (1975), Mitchell argued that women's role in the foundation of civilisation was quite unlike that of their brothers: men exchanged women, women were the objects of men's exchange. The initial relations of exchange between groups of men, understood through the insights of the Freudian Oedipal drama, formed the very foundations of human language and culture. Fourteen years after Mitchell published her influential book, Pateman (1988a; 1988b) used some of the same conceptual building blocks to rewrite conventional speculative histories of a much more recent event. Rather than place the Oedipal drama at the very beginning of human civilisation, Pateman used Freud's account to reinterpret the debate between proponents of the social contract and the defenders of absolutism in the late seventeenth century. And while Mitchell posited a fundamental *continuity* of patriarchal rule, a transhistorical 'law of the father', Pateman outlined a radical *discontinuity* between paternal and fraternal forms of patriarchy. The victory of social contract theorists over those who defended patriarchalist absolutist rule, she argued, gave birth to a new 'fraternal' political entity; the defeat of the rule of fathers ushered in a rule of the victorious brothers. As in Mitchell's account, women were not *party to the social contract*; they were its *subject*.

In classical patriarchy, Pateman noted, society was structured by kinship, and men governed as fathers. After the political defeat of patriarchalism in eighteenth-century Europe, men came to govern women as members of a fraternity. The social contract between free and equal brothers, Pateman argued, was not only built around the categorical exclusion of women from the 'body politic', it was premised on a submerged sex-right, or men's orderly access to women's bodies. Pateman acknowledged that these foundational premises were not explicitly stated by any of the social contract theorists, but believed that they could be brought into sharp relief if viewed through Freud's account of the original patricide as outlined in *Moses and Monotheism* (1939) and *Totem and Taboo* (1913).

Despite their lack of alternatives, Pateman argued, women might well enter the marriage contract freely. Once married, however, they become subject to the patriarchal right of their husbands. This is because the marriage contract (modelled as it is on Roman law) mandates that women exchange 'protection' for obedience, labour and irrevocable sexual access to their bodies. In turn, because of the unique and irrevocably subordinate position of women in the private sphere of the family, women and men cannot be civil equals. In both law and political thought, the 'individual' is a patriarchal category which by definition excludes women: he is a man who makes use of a woman's body as his sexual property.

But what is the status of this account, particularly as couched in terms of Freud's colourful stories? Pateman argues that beginning in the seventeenth century, when stories of the original contract were first told, men set up novel forms of practical everyday domination through telling a new conjectural story of human achievements. While the story of the social contract is merely a political fiction – and the use of Oedipal imagery an ironical symbolic device to dramatise it – this discursive event was also a momentous and lasting intervention in the political world. Not only does public imagery contain powerful references to the male birthing of polities, esteemed public traditions and institutions; contractual relations today are widely seen as paths to justice and freedom; the all-pervasive current emphases on individual initiative, privatisation, and attacks on state services, all testify to their undiminished significance. In turn, Pateman believed, her excavation of the full story of the social contract has transformative political implications.

The Sexual Contract became the subject of wide-ranging debates. Some critics pointed out that a discursive interpretation of social contract debates seems to be overwritten on earlier drafts of the book where texts and social history were more closely intertwined, philosophers' words had direct social consequences, and interpretations of the sexual contract provided a straightforward key to contemporary social relations. Pateman's work also inspired much fruitful new scholarship, including work on what the philosopher Charles Mills (1997) called the racial contract (see also Pateman and Mills 2007). In recognition of its importance, in 2005 the book received a prestigious award for work of 'exceptional quality by a living political theorist that is still considered significant after a time span of at least 15 years since the original publication'.

Historically specific, messy patriarchies

The weak point of Pateman's account – the messy dynamics of historically specific local patriarchies – became the focus of much other scholarship. The US political scientist Cynthia Enloe and the British sociologist Cynthia Cockburn, for example, use patriarchy as a useful reminder that they are talking about relations of power; 'to remind us that it's something big and systemic we're dealing with here' (Cock-burn 2003). However, they also portray patriarchy as messy and full of contradictions, subject to far-reaching struggles, and constantly needing all sorts of maintenance to keep it going.

In a recent interview (Cohn and Enloe 2003), Enloe described how she was mortified when, as a newly self-conscious feminist, she realised her book's manuscript contained only two mentions of women, and terrified when, in 1980, a senior colleague told feminist conference participants 'We have to talk about patriarchy'. Today, she noted, she could not imagine trying to think seriously about the constructions of power and the systems by which power is both perpetuated and implemented without talking about patriarchy. Remembering how scary the term sounded to her, she tries to provide a lot of examples in her detailed work on topics such as the British House of Commons, textile companies, the Israeli military, Chilean political parties, and Bosnia's and Afghanistan's new governments. Patriarchy, she adds, 'is not a sledge hammer being swung around a raving feminist head. It is a tool; it sheds light at the same time as it reveals patterns of causality'. She keeps using the concept because 'it reminds us that we're investigating power'. She then defines patriarchy not as a pre-existing structure making people do things, but as a network of unequal social relations that delimits people's actions but is full of glitches and contradictions and has to be constantly patched up:

> It is not men on top that makes something patriarchal. It's men who are recognized and claim a certain form of masculinity, for the sake of being more valued, more 'serious', and 'the protectors of/ and controllers of those people who are less 'masculine' that makes any organization, any community, any society patriarchal. It's never automatic; it's rarely self-perpetuating. It takes daily tending. It takes decisions – even if those are masked as 'tradition'. It relies on many women finding patriarchal relationships comfortable, sometimes rewarding.
>
> *(Cohn and Enloe 2003: 1192)*

Not least because of the unpredictability and variability of social relations, Enloe is especially influenced by feminist-informed, historically minded ethnography, and tries to assemble accounts of what would later be called 'total social division of labour'.

In her work on armies and wars, for example, Enloe (1983) shows how militarism and the military affect everyone. Women are involved as military wives, soldiers' mothers and sisters, prostitutes, entertainers, cleaners, workers in munitions factories, civilian casualties, supporters of military campaigns or anti-war activists, and more recently as soldiers themselves. Patriarchy is there as a background force making sense of complex developments, but is full of contradictions, and always an achievement in the making. 'What becomes surprisingly clear, as one examines these military processes', Enloe (1983: 213) notes, 'is that the military is often very confused'. True to her word, Enloe uses the concept sparingly; around once in nineteen pages in both *Does Khaki Become You* and *Bananas, Beaches and Bases* (1989).

The British feminist sociologist and peace activist Cynthia Cockburn thinks with patriarchy in a similar way. As she recently noted, 'Some women use the term "patriarchy" to describe the kind of man-dominated "gender order" we currently live in'. Cockburn agreed such a short-hand term was really useful in reminding us 'that it's something big and systemic we're dealing with here'. But this did not mean that this big and systematic social arrangement (which could also be called an exploitative gender order) was always and everywhere the same:

> Of course, the gender order is always intertwined with a social class order, an ethnic order and other facets of power in society. In addition, there's a neat term: 'gender regime'. It means the gender arrangements in any given institution. It prompts us to ask useful questions like: how does gender power work in the boardroom of multinational? or, what are the gender relations of my child's sec-ondary school? We'd expect all these to have interestingly different gender regimes.
>
> *(Cockburn 2003: 6)*

Interestingly different gender regimes

In the 1970s, even those feminists who saw patriarchy as one trans-historical system noted that it looked a bit different in different times and places, and for women from different social groups. A decade later, researchers completed detailed studies with titles such as 'Patriarchy in Colonial New England' (Folbre 1980); 'Peasant Patriarchy and the Subversion of the Collective in Vietnam' (Wiegersma 1991); 'Not So Much a Factory, More a Form of Patriarchy: Gender and Class during Industrialisation' (Lown 1983); and *Infertility and Patriarchy: The Cultural Politics of Gender and Family Life in Egypt* (Inhorn 1996). In contemporary Europe, the British social geographer Simon Duncan stressed, there were significant differences in gender inequality at regional and local scales, produced and defined as much by regional and local processes of economic development and cultural understanding as they are by national level processes centred around the welfare state. It followed that regions and not just countries are likely to have different types of 'gender contracts', making for 'differentiated patriarchy' (Duncan 1994; 1995: 265).

Employing the concept of patriarchy to think through similar issues, many writers published work on the complicated *relationships between* a range of 'local patriarchies', and focussed on *transitions* from one form of patriarchy to another. Stacey, for example, charted transitions from Confucian patriarchy to New Democratic patriarchy and then patriarchal socialism in *Patriarchy and Socialist Revolution in China* (1983); Besse tackled *Restructuring Patriarchy: The Modernization of Gender Inequality in Brazil, 1914–1945* (1996), and Hodgson wrote about 'Pastoralism, Patriarchy and History: Changing Gender Relations among Maasai in Tanganyika, 1890–1940' (1999). Focussing on the modern West, Brown described a shift from private to public patriarchy in her often cited essay, 'Mothers, Fathers and Children: From Private to Public Patriarchy' (1981); a number of writers tackled patriarchy in transition from feudalism to capitalism.

The Canadian sociologist Wally Seccombe drew on work such as this in his *A Millennium of Family Change: Feudalism to Capitalism in Northwestern Europe* (1992) and *Weathering the Storm: Working-Class Families from the Industrial Revolution to the Fertility Decline* (1993). His particular emphasis was on the interplay between the complex dynamics of different family forms and changing forms of production. In families of peasant households, for example, wives had authority over both female and male servants and apprentices, parents disciplined children through discretionary allocation of inheritance, and young people had to wait for parents' consent before they could marry. In protoindustrial or cottage industry households, in contrast, young people's inheritance was the skill they acquired as they assisted with production. As highly skilled workers, young women had considerable bargaining power. Here, parents grew rich with children's assistance, and became poor as daughters and sons left home to set up their own households. In turn, particular patterns of family formation, such as late and non-universal marriage in Northwestern Europe, could facilitate rapid industrialisation.

In an overlapping project, the Australian historical sociologist Pavla Miller's *Transformations of Patriarchy in the West, 1500–1900* (1998) combined the focus on family formation and the way production was organised with an account of the process of state formation. Influenced by Pateman, and focussing on changing forms of familial, economic and political modes of patriarchal governance, the book traces the uneven and conflict-ridden rise and fall of a patriarchalist social order and its replacement by fraternal forms of governance. A key theme of the book concerns attempts by various reformers to instil self-mastery, originally expected of monks and masters, into ordinary people. Impressive schemes of social control, Miller concludes, rarely worked as their promoters imagined they should; different aspects of patriarchy were transformed at different paces at different times; uneven development and regional variations make nonsense of any attempts to organise history into orderly and exclusive stages.

Seccombe and Miller attempted to understand the engine of social change in all its messy and thunderous force. In her extensive work, the British sociologist Sylvia Walby set out to tidy the mess, and produce a systematic and comprehensive template of feminist theory. Different forms of patriarchy, she argued in *Theorising Patriarchy* (1990), arise from different combinations of more or less intense male domination of women through six key patriarchal structures: the patriarchal (domestic) mode of production; patriarchal relations in paid work; patriarchal relations in the state; male violence; patriarchal relations in sexuality; and patriarchal relations in cultural institutions including religion, media and education. In recent Western history, Walby argues, these structures combine into two basic types of patriarchy. *Private patriarchy*, which peaked in Britain in the mid-nineteenth century, is based upon the household, with a patriarch controlling women individually and directly in the relatively private sphere of the home. More recently, *public patriarchy* became dominant. While the household may still be a significant patriarchal site, it is institutions conventionally regarded as part of the public domain which are central in the maintenance of public patriarchy. In order to distinguish between different industrialised countries, Walby further divides public patriarchy into two: one where the market and the other where the state plays the major role in bringing women into the public sphere.

In subsequent work, Walby (1994) made a further distinction between the form and the degree of patriarchy. The form of patriarchy refers to the relationship between the different elements of patriarchy, for instance whether or not women have widespread access to full-time paid work during their adult lives. Public and private patriarchy represent two overall forms. The degree of patriarchy refers to the intensity or extent by which women are subordinated to men, for instance the level of wage inequality between women and men. This scheme, according to Walby, 'creates the theoretical space to avoid ethnocentrism in comparative analysis, since a particular form is no longer necessarily associated with a particular degree of inequality'. While colleagues have appreciated the many valuable insights of Walby's work, many questioned her systematising approach. Ever more complicated pigeonholes, critics note, do not fix the problem of building one's analysis around fixed, transhistorical categories. More recently, Walby (2007) stopped using the concept of patriarchy, but continued mapping European gender regimes. In order to systematise accounts of gender inequality, she now employs intersectionality and complexity theory as organising frameworks.

Many other projects charted differently gendered social arrangements, but did not employ the concept of patriarchy to do so. The journal *Social Politics*, for example, was set up in 1994 as a forum to illuminate the gendered dimensions of social policy and citizenship, and examine the role of states in constructing and organising gender relations in the family, workplace and society, and the complicated flows of economic resources, caring work and emotions among household members and in society as a whole, at a time when all these were being renegotiated and recast (The Editors 1994). Since then, the journal has published extensive debates on gendered welfare state regimes, different types of maternalism, and global chains of care work. It continues to trace 'gendered transformations of governance, economy, and citizenship'. As the editors of a special issue on this topic put it:

> We are concerned to identify and examine the new times and new spaces being revealed in contemporary feminist and gender-sensitive research, and the ways in which these problematize familiar understandings of gender, sexuality, and femininity. For example, new forms of governance, financialization, and changing forms of community organization have all reconfigured conventional understandings of relationships between the state and the market, production and social reproduction, men and women, sex and gender, here and there. Second, we are concerned to trace the new questions that have emerged as scholars have redeployed the analytical tools provided by feminist theory in new domains.
>
> *(Larner* et al. *2013: 157)*

War over the family

The difficult issues feminists in the 1970s tackled by thinking with patriarchy cut across deeply held convictions and the fabric of people's everyday lives. Critiques of 'the family' turned out to be one of the most hotly debated and contentious issues confronting women's movements. Despite wide theoretical and strategic differences, one issue tended to unite early second-wave feminists and their New Left contemporaries: an implacable opposition to what they called the bourgeois patriarchal family, or the family as an institution (see for example Barrett and McIntosh 1982). Whether the family oppressed women and children through crippling sex-role socialisation, as one of the key ideological capitalist state apparatuses, as a vestige of the feudal mode of production, through the internal machine of the Oedipal drama, or else through physical violence and the expropriation of women's productive and reproductive labour – or all of the above – it stood in the path of women's liberation. It followed that for women to be liberated, 'the family, as that term is presently understood, must go'; perhaps women should also be liberated from the care of children, possibly even from the begetting of babies. To many activists, current family crises should be celebrated as the harbinger of more humane and equitable social relations; those who argued that the family was changing rather than dying were denounced as defenders of patriarchy (see for example Breines *et al.* 1978).

Principled denunciations of the family as the fulcrum of oppression seriously annoyed those who experienced the family as a 'haven in a heartless word', a focus of community resistance to racism and class oppression, or simply the most affordable way to live and bring up children – as well as those for whom family reunion was a fragile victory against hostile immigration officials. As the going got tough in the 1980s and 1990s, many underprivileged and disenfranchised groups intensified their reliance on family networks. Commenting on life in the US in the 1980s, the sociologist Judith Stacey (1987: 10) noted that:

> In the emerging class structure, marriage is becoming a major axis of stratification because it structures access to a second income. The married female as 'secondary' wage-earner lifts a former working-class or middle-class family into comparative affluence, while the loss or lack of access to a male income can force women and their children into poverty.

In a climate such as this, the historical 'non-necessity of family', which Mitchell predicted in her *Psychoanalysis and Feminism* in 1975, receded into the distance (Simons 1979: 392).

In the UK, the sociologist Valerie Amos and the filmmaker Pratibha Parmar (1984) pointed out angrily that 'in identifying the institution of the family as a source of oppression for women, white feminists have again revealed their cultural and racial myopia'. This was because 'the British state through its immigration legislation has done all it can to destroy the Asian family by separating husbands from wives, wives from husbands and parents from children'. Many white feminists also stated they 'found it very difficult to accept arranged marriages, which they saw as reactionary'. Amos and Parmar (1984: 15) responded that 'it is not up to them to accept or reject arranged marriages but up to us to challenge, accept, or reform, depending on our various perspectives, on our own terms and in our own culturally specific ways'.[2] Parita Trivedi agreed that the last thing members of her community would do is ask for state intervention on their behalf; 'to ally and collude with the racist state in a pseudo-feminist struggle would be crass and misguided'. Distrust of the state is well-founded, she noted:

> There are various ways in which innumerable Asian families have been divided by the operations of immigration regulations; children have been separated from parents and elderly parents from their main supporters. Reuniting people of a particular family and attempting to overthrow the racist legislation have been important struggles for Asian women ... The particular Asian family form has been systematically under attack by the state not only through the workings of immigration rules, but also in other ideological ways, for example through the media and by welfare administrators who characterize the Asian families as being pathological.
>
> *(Trivedi 1984: 46–47)*

In Australia, critiques of 'the family' additionally came up against the violent history of white colonisation. The *National Inquiry into the Separation of Aboriginal and Torres Strait Islander Children from Their Families*, completed in 1997, for example estimated that between one in three and one in ten Indigenous children were forcibly removed from their families in the period between 1910 and 1970. This practice, the Commission noted, affected the identity of Indigenous Australians in profound ways. It disorganised many people's sense of coherence: their notions of who they were, how they fitted into the world and where they were going. It also destroyed the sense of worth of being Aboriginal and fragmented the sense of identity both of those who were taken away and of the families who were left behind. Indeed, 'the loss of so many of their children has affected the efficacy and morale of many Indigenous communities ... the child-rearing function of whole communities was undermined and denied, particularly where all children were required to live in mission dormitories'. The *Inquiry* concluded that 'when a child was forcibly removed that child's entire community lost, often permanently, its chance to perpetuate itself in that child ... this was a primary objective of forcible removals and it is the reason they amount to genocide' (Commonwealth of Australia 1997: 190).

The place of matriarchy and patriarchy in African American history was another deeply contentious issue. Racial denigration of slaves typically included stereotypes of emasculated black men and unnaturally powerful black women. In the twentieth century, scholarly works on Black American families drew on these stereotypes to identify a black 'matriarchate' as one of the major sources of black inferiority. It followed that civilised patriarchy would cure the malaise of the black family, and produce an appropriate differentiation between the roles of women and men. One of the most influential works along these lines was Daniel Moynihan's 1965 report for the US Department of Labor, *The Negro Family: The Case for National Action*. Poor and working-class black families and communities, the Report declared, were unlike the rest of white patriarchal America and therefore doomed to live life in a 'tangle of pathology'. According to Moynihan, black female dominance 'seriously retards the progress' of blacks as a race; the strength of black women was an 'instrument of castration' of black men. In response to racist texts saying that matriarchy caused the degeneration of black families, generations of anti-racist scholars felt compelled to provide evidence of the 'normal heterosexuality and patriarchal manhood' of black gender relations (Richardson 2003). A few adopted the opposite approach. In theorisations of *Négritude*, they valorised the supposed matriarchal bases of Pan-African heritage. The Senegalese historian and Pan-Africanist, Cheikh Anta Diop, and following him the Nigerian-born anthropologist Ifi Amadiume, for example argued that matriarchy constituted a unifying African moral code and culture until it was gradually destabilised by patriarchal 'outsiders' such as Islamic Arabs and Christian Europeans (Diop 1959; Amadiume 1997).

By the late 1990s, critiques such as these were accepted by most feminist activists, and have become a commonplace of feminist scholarship. During the same period, New Right politicians and fundamentalist religious organisations intensified claims that feminism weakened healthy patriarchal relations between women and men, and undermined family values. Single mothers and same sex couples became the target of particularly vicious attacks; a wide range of family services were abolished or scaled back. Domestic violence, and inequitable distribution of household work, time and resources continued, as did gender discrimination at work. New wars flared up, and global chains of care work complicated analyses of gender divisions of labour. Feminists now tend to mobilise against injustices in ways which are respectful of community diversity; most avoid using the concept of patriarchy in their analyses and campaigns. Anti-feminist activists, in contrast, often call for the restoration of a civilised, white Western patriarchy as the solution to deep social problems. The terms of the debate have changed, but the war over the family continues.

Notes

1 The quote on rules is from Alexander and Taylor (1981: 370–371).
2 In 1997, Valerie Amos was elevated to the peerage as Baroness Amos. In 2015, the former politician and senior UN official was appointed Director of the School of Oriental and African Studies at the University of London.

References

Adkins, Lisa and Diana Leonard (2005) 'Reconstructing French Feminism: Commodification, materialism and sex', Ch. 1 in Diana Leonard and Lisa Adkins (eds) *Sex in Question: French materialist feminism*. Taylor & Francis e-Library.

Ahmed, Leila (1992) *Women and Gender in Islam: Historical roots of a modern debate*. New Haven, CT: Yale University Press.

Alexander, Leslie M. (2004) 'The Challenge of Race: Rethinking the position of Black women in the field of women's history', *Journal of Women's History* 16(4): 50–60.

Alexander, Sally and Barbara Taylor (1981) 'In Defence of "Patriarchy"', in Raphael Samuel (ed.) *People's History and Socialist Theory*. London: Routledge and Kegan Paul, pp. 370–374.

Amadiume, Ife (1997) 'Theorising Matriarchy in Africa: Kinship ideologies and systems in Africa and Europe', Ch. 3 in *Reinventing Africa: Matriarchy, religion and culture*. London and New York: Zed Books, pp. 71–88.

Amos, Valerie and Pratibha Parmar (1984) 'Challenging Imperial Feminism', *Feminist Review* 17: 'Many Voices, One Chant: Black Feminist Perspectives' (Autumn): 3–19.

Atkinson, Jane Monnig (1982) 'Anthropology', *Signs* 8(2): 236–258.

Barrett, Michèle (1992) 'Words and Things: Materialism and method in feminist analysis', in Michèle Barrett and Anne Phillips (eds) *Destabilizing Theory: Contemporary feminist debates*. Cambridge: Polity Press, pp. 201–219.

Barrett, Michèle and Mary McIntosh (1982) *The Anti-Social Family*. London: Verso.

Bennett, Judith (2006) *History Matters: Patriarchy and the challenge of feminism.* Philadelphia: University of Pennsylvania Press, pp. 21–22.

Besse, Susan (1996) *Restructuring Patriarchy: The modernization of gender inequality in Brazil, 1914–1945.* Chapel Hill: University of North Carolina Press.

Boydston, Jeanne (2008) 'Gender as a Question of Historical Analysis', *Gender and History* 20(3): 558–583.

Breines, Wini, Margaret Cerullo and Judith Stacey (1978) 'Social Biology, Family Studies, and Antifeminist Backlash', *Feminist Studies* 4(1): 43–67.

Brown, Carol (1981) 'Mothers, Fathers and Children: From private to public patriarchy', in Lydia Sargent (ed.) *Women and Revolution.* Boston, MA: South End Press.

Butler, Judith and Joan Scott (eds) (1992) 'Introduction', in *Feminists Theorise the Political.* New York: Routledge, pp. xiii–xvii.

Carsten, Janet (ed.) (2000) *Cultures of Relatedness: New approaches to the study of kinship.* Cambridge: Cambridge University Press.

Carsten, Janet (ed.) (2003) *After Kinship.* Cambridge: Cambridge University Press.

Causey, Ann S. (2003) 'Ecofeminism', in Marci Bortman, Peter Brimblecombe and Mary Ann Cunningham (eds) *Environmental Encyclopaedia*, vol. 1, 3rd edn. Detroit, MI: Gale, pp. 412–413.

Chakrabarty, Dipesh (2000) *Provincializing Europe: Postcolonial thought and historical difference*, Princeton, NJ: Princeton University Press.

Chodorow, Nancy (1989) *Feminism and Psychoanalytic Theory.* New Haven, CT: Yale University Press, pp. 1–19.

Cockburn, Cynthia (2003) 'Why (and Which) Feminist Antimilitarism?' Article based on a talk given by the author at the Annual General Meeting of the Women's International League for Peace and Freedom, Nantwich, 1 March 2003. www.ikff.se/wordpress/wp-content/uploads/2013/02/Blogfemantimilitarism.pdf, accessed 11 September 2016.

Cohn, Carol and Cynthia Enloe (2003) 'A Conversation with Cynthia Enloe: Feminists look at masculinity and the men who wage war', *Signs* 28(4): 1187–1207.

Collins, Patricia Hill and Sirma Bilge (2016) *Intersectionality.* Oxford: Polity Press.

Commonwealth of Australia, Human Rights and Equal Opportunity Commission (1997) *Bringing them Home: Report of the National Inquiry into the Separation of Aboriginal and Torres Strait Islander Children from Their Families.* Sydney: HREOC.

Connell, Raewyn (2007) *Southern Theory: The global dynamics of knowledge in social science.* Sydney: Allen and Unwin.

Connell, Raewyn W. (2011) 'Sociology Has a World History', Ch. 7 in *Confronting Equality: Gender, knowledge and social change.* Sydney: Allen and Unwin, pp. 103–118.

Delphy, Christine (1995) 'The Invention of French Feminism: An essential move', *Yale French Studies* 87: 190–221.

Diop, Cheikh Anta (1959) *The Cultural Unity of Black Africa: The domains of matriarchy and patriarchy in classical antiquity.* Chicago, IL: Third World Press.

Donovan, Sarah K. (2016) 'Luce Irigaray', in *The Internet Encyclopedia of Philosophy.* ISSN 2161–0002, www.iep.utm.edu/irigaray, accessed 26 September 2016.

Duncan, Simon (1994) 'Theorising Differences in Patriarchy', *Environment and Planning A* 26(8): 1177–1194.

Duncan, Simon (1995) 'Theorising European Gender Systems', *Journal of European Social Policy* 5(4): 263–284.

Enloe, Cynthia (1983) *Does Khaki Become You? The militarisation of women's lives.* London: Pluto Press.

Enloe, Cynthia (1989) *Bananas, Beaches and Bases: Making feminist sense of international politics.* London: Pandora Press.

Folbre, Nancy (1980) 'Patriarchy in Colonial New England', *Review of Radical Political Economics* 12(2): 4–13.

French, Marilyn (1977) *The Women's Room.* New York: Summit Books.

French, Marilyn (2002) *From Eve to Dawn: A History of women in the world.* Toronto: McArthur.

Freud, Sigmund (1913) *Totem and Taboo.* Boston, MA: Beacon Press.

Freud, Sigmund (1939) *Moses and Monotheism.* New York: A. A. Knopf.

Ghodsee, Kristen (2010) 'Revisiting the United Nations Decade for Women: Brief reflections on feminism, capitalism and Cold War politics in the early years of the international women's movement', *Women's Studies International Forum* 33(1): 3–12.

Grosz, Elizabeth (1989) *Sexual Subversions: Three French feminists.* Sydney: Allen & Unwin.

Guy-Sheftall, Beverly (2008) 'Women's Studies: A view from the margins', in Alice E. Ginsberg (ed.) *The Evolution of American Women's Studies: Reflections on triumphs, controversies, and change.* Basingstoke: Palgrave Macmillan, pp. 103–115.

Helly, Dorothy O. and Susan M. Reverby (1992) *Gendered Domains: Rethinking public and private in women's history.* Ithaca, NY: Cornell University Press.

Hobson, Janell (ed.) (2016) *Are All the Women Still White? Rethinking race, expanding feminisms.* Albany: State University of New York Press.

Hodgson, Dorothy L. (1999) 'Pastoralism, Patriarchy and History: Changing gender relations among Maasai in Tanganyika, 1890–1940', *Journal of African History* 40(1): 41–65.

Huggins, Jackie (1994) 'A Contemporary View of Aboriginal Women's Relationship to the White Women's Movement', in Norma Grieve and Ailsa Burns (eds) *Australian Women: Contemporary feminist thought.* Melbourne: Oxford University Press, pp. 70–79.

Hull, Gloria T., Patricia Bell Scott and Barbara Smith (eds) (1982) *All the Women Are White, All the Blacks Are Men, But Some of Us Are Brave: Black women's studies*. New York: The Feminist Press.

Inhorn, Marcia C. (1996) *Infertility and Patriarchy: The cultural politics of gender and family life in Egypt*. Philadelphia: University of Pennsylvania Press.

Irigaray, Luce (1985) *Speculum of the Other Woman*, Translated by Gillian C. Gill. Ithaca, NY: Cornell University Press.

Irigaray, Luce (ed.) (2008) *Luce Irigaray: Teaching (1)*. London: Continuum ProQuest ebrary. Accessed 13 August 2016.

Irigaray, Luce and Stephen Pluháček (2008) *Conversations*. London: Continuum eBook Collection (EBSCOhost), accessed 13 August 2016.

Jaggar, Alison and Paula Rothenberg (1978) *Feminist Frameworks: Alternative theoretical accounts of the relations between women and men*. New York: McGraw-Hill.

Jaggar, Alison and Paula Rothenberg (1993) *Feminist Frameworks: Alternative theoretical accounts of the relations between women and men*. New York: McGraw-Hill.

James, Stanlie M., Frances Smith Foster and Beverly Guy-Sheftall (eds) (2009) *Still Brave: The evolution of Black women's studies*. New York: Feminist Press.

Kandiyoti, Deniz (1988) 'Bargaining with Patriarchy', *Gender and Society* 2(3): 274–290.

Kandiyoti, Deniz (1998) 'Gender, Power and Contestation: Rethinking bargaining with patriarchy', in C. Jackson and R. Pearson (eds) *Feminist Visions of Development*. London: Routledge, pp. 135–151.

Kemp, Sandra and Judith Squires (1997) *Feminisms*. Oxford and New York: Oxford University Press.

Kirkley, Debra L. (2000) 'Is Motherhood Good for Women? A feminist exploration', *Journal of Obstetric, Gynecologic and Neonatal Nursing* 29(5): 459–464.

Lake, Marilyn (2003) 'Woman, Black, Indigenous: Recognition struggles in dialogue', Ch. 6 in Barbara Hobson (ed.) *Recognition Struggles and Social Movements: Cultural claims, contested identities, power and agency*. Cambridge: Cambridge University Press, pp. 145–187.

Landes, Joan (ed.) (1998) *Feminism, the Public and the Private*. Oxford: Oxford University Press.

Larner, Wendy, Maria Fannin, Julie MacLeavy and Wenfei Winnie Wang (2013) 'Introduction: Gendered transformations of governance, economy, and citizenship', *Social Politics* 20(2): 157–164.

Lerner, Gerda (1986) *The Creation of Patriarchy*. New York: Oxford University Press.

Lerner, Gerda (1993) *The Creation of Feminist Consciousness*. Oxford: Oxford University Press.

Lown, Judy (1983) 'Not So Much a Factory, More a Form of Patriarchy: Gender and class during industrialisation', in E. Gamarnikov, D. Morgan, J. Purvis and D. Taylorson (eds) *Gender, Class and Work*. London: Heinemann.

Mama, Amina (1984) 'Black Women, the Economic Crisis and the British State', *Feminist Review* 17: 21–35.

Mani, Lata (1998) *Contentious Traditions: The debate on sati in colonial India*. London: University of California Press.

May, Vivian M. (2015) *Pursuing Intersectionality, Unsettling dominant imaginaries*. New York: Routledge.

Mayo, Katherine (2000) *Mother India*, ed. Mrinalini Sinha. Ann Arbor: University of Michigan Press.

McCall, Leslie (2005) 'The Complexity of Intersectionality', *Signs* 30(3): 1771–1800.

Messer-Davidow, Ellen (2002) *Disciplining Feminism: From social activism to academic discourse*. Durham, NC: Duke University Press.

Miller, Pavla (1998) *Transformations of Patriarchy in the West, 1500–1900*. Bloomington: Indiana University Press.

Mills, Charles W. (1997) *The Racial Contract*. Ithaca, NY: Cornell University Press.

Mitchell, Juliet (1975) *Psychoanalysis and Feminism*. London: Penguin.

Mitchell, Juliet (2000) *Psychoanalysis and Feminism*. Reprinted with a new introduction. London: Penguin.

Mohanty, Chandra Talpade (1988) 'Under Western Eyes: Feminist scholarship and colonial discourses', *Feminist Review* 30: 61–88.

Mohanty, Chandra Talpade (2003) '"Under Western Eyes" Revisited: Feminist solidarity through anticapitalist struggles', *Signs* 28(2): 499–535.

Moi, Toril (1989) 'Feminist, Female, Feminine', in Catherine Belsey and Jane Moore (eds) *The Feminist Reader: Essays in gender and the politics of literary criticism*. London: Macmillan, pp. 117–132.

Moran, Mary H. (2010) 'Gender, Militarism, and Peace-Building', *Annual Review of Anthropology* 39: 261–274.

Narayan, Uma (1997) 'Cross-Cultural Connections, Border-Crossings, and "Death by Culture": Thinking about dowry-murders in India and domestic-violence murders in the United States', in *Dislocating Cultures: Identities, traditions and Third World feminisms*. London: Taylor & Francis, pp. 81–117.

Ortner, Sherry B. (1996) 'Making Gender: Toward a feminist, minority, post-colonial, subaltern, etc., theory of practice', Ch. 1 in *Making Gender: The politics and erotics of culture*. Boston, MA: Beacon Press.

Pateman, Carole (1988a) *The Sexual Contract*. Cambridge: Polity Press.

Pateman, Carole (1988b) 'The Fraternal Social Contract: Some observations on patriarchal civil society', in John Keane (ed.) *Civil Society and the State: New European perspectives*. London: Verso.

Pateman, Carole and Charles W. Mills (2007) *Contract and Domination*. Cambridge: Polity Press.

Plumwood, Val (1993) *Feminism and the Mastery of Nature*. London and New York: Routledge.

Plumwood, Val (1994) 'The Ecopolitics Debate and the Politics of Nature', in Karen J. Warren (ed.) *Ecological Feminism*. London and New York: Routledge, pp. 64–87.

Rafael, Adeline R. F. (1996) 'Power and Caring: A dialectic in nursing', *Advances in Nursing Science* 19(1): 3–17.

Rich, Adrienne (1986) *Of Woman Born: Motherhood as experience and institution*. 10th anniversary edition with a new foreword. New York and London: Norton and Virago.

Richardson, Mattie Udora (2003) 'No More Secrets, No More Lies: African American history and compulsory heterosexuality', *Journal of Women's History* 15(3): 63–76.

Rothenberg, Paula (2008) 'Women Studies: The early years: when sisterhood was powerful', in Alice E. Ginsberg (ed.) *The Evolution of American Women's Studies: Reflections on triumphs, controversies, and change*. New York: Palgrave Macmillan, pp. 67–86.

Rubin, Gayle (2011) *Deviations: Essays in sex, gender, and politics*. Durham, NC: Duke University Press.

Rupp, Leila J. (2008) 'Revisiting Patriarchy', *Journal of Women's History* 20(2): 136–140.

Scharff, Christina (2012) *Repudiating Feminism: Young women in a neoliberal world*. Farnham: Ashgate.

Scott, Joan (1986) 'Gender: A useful category of historical analysis', *American Historical Review* 91(5): 1053–1075.

Scott, Joan Wallach and Debra Keates (eds) (2004) *Going Public: Feminism and the shifting boundaries of the private sphere*. Urbana: University of Illinois Press.

Seccombe, Wally (1992) *A Millennium of Family Change: Feudalism to capitalism in Northwestern Europe*. London: Verso.

Seccombe, Wally (1993) *Weathering the Storm: Working-class families from the industrial revolution to the fertility decline*. London: Verso.

Sewell, William H. Jr (2005) *Logics of History: Social theory and social transformation*. Chicago, IL: University of Chicago Press.

Silverman, Eric K. (2004) 'Anthropology and Circumcision', *Annual Review of Anthropology* 33: 419–445.

Simons, Margaret A. (1979) 'Racism and Feminism: A schism in the sisterhood', *Feminist Studies* 5(2): 384–401.

Spivak, Gayatri Chakravorty (1985) 'Can the Subaltern Speak? Speculations on widow sacrifice', *Wedge* 7–8: 120–130.

Stacey, Judith (1983) *Patriarchy and Socialist Revolution in China*. Berkeley: University of California Press.

Stacey, Judith (1987) 'Sexism by a Subtler Name? Post-industrial conditions and postfeminist consciousness in the Silicon Valley', *Socialist Review* 96: 341–361.

Stacey, Judith (2000) 'Is Academic Feminism an Oxymoron?', *Signs* 25(4): 1189–1194.

Stewart, Mary (2010) 'Feminisms and Intrapartum Care', Ch. 15 in Denis Walsh and Soo Downe (eds) *Essential Midwifery Practice: Intrapartum care*. Chichester: Wiley-Blackwell, pp. 275–288. eBook Collection (EBSCOhost). Accessed 14 August 2016.

Stone, Alison (2006) *Luce Irigaray and the Philosophy of Sexual Difference*. Cambridge: Cambridge University Press.

The Editors (1994) 'Introduction', *Social Politics* 1(1): 1–3.

Thornton, Margaret (ed.) (1995) *Public and Private: Feminist legal debates*. Melbourne: Oxford University Press.

Tong, Rosemarie (1998) *Feminist Thought: A more comprehensive introduction*. 2nd edn. Sydney: Allen and Unwin.

Trivedi, Parita (1984) 'To Deny Our Fullness: Asian women in the making of history', *Feminist Review* 17: 37–50.

Tyson, Lois (2014) 'Feminist Criticism', Ch. 4 in *Critical Theory Today: A user-friendly guide*. 3rd edn. New York: Routledge, pp. 79–128.

Walby, Sylvia (1990) *Theorising Patriarchy*. Oxford: Basil Blackwell.

Walby, Sylvia (1994) 'Methodological and Theoretical Issues in the Comparative Analysis of Gender Relations in Western Europe', *Environment and Planning A* 26(9): 1339–1354.

Walby, Sylvia (2007) 'Complexity Theory, Systems Theory and Multiple Intersecting Social Inequalities', *Philosophy of the Social Sciences* 37(4): 449–470.

Walley, Christine J. (1997) 'Searching for "Voices": Feminism, anthropology, and the global debate over female genital operations', *Cultural Anthropology* 12(3): 405–438.

Warren, Karen J. (1993) 'A Feminist Philosophical Perspective on Ecofeminist Spiritualities', in Carol J. Adams (ed.) *Ecofeminism and the Sacred*. New York: Continuum.

Warren, Karen J. (ed.) (1994) *Ecological Feminism*. London and New York: Routledge.

Wiegersma, Nan (1991) 'Peasant Patriarchy and the Subversion of the Collective in Vietnam', *Review of Radical Political Economics* 23 (3+4): 174–197.

7

CONTESTING PATRIARCHY TODAY

The beginning of the new millennium saw deepening interdependence across the world, continued de-industrialisation in the global North, and accelerating industrialisation in some regions of the global South. In Europe, North America and Australia, old industrial centres turned into rustbelts. Jobs and careers became less secure; many were casualised and redesigned to require lower levels of skill; others were simply paid less. Increasing proportions of women joined the paid workforce. Even if they managed to keep their jobs, many male 'breadwinners' no longer earned what came to be regarded as comfortable family incomes, or even enough to pay pressing bills. In many regions and industries, the privileges previously accorded to men and to whites were whittled away. Families continued to change. In the US in the 2000s, around half of all marriages ended in divorce; in the UK four in ten, and in Australia one in three. Many more mothers were raising children alone; economists began describing a new 'feminisation of poverty'. Alarmed about the decline of 'traditional families', others sounded alarm about a crisis of fatherhood. As one particularly influential US commentator put it:

> Fatherlessness is the most harmful demographic trend of this generation. It is the leading cause of declining child well-being in our

society. It is also the engine driving our most urgent social problems, from crime to adolescent pregnancy to child sexual abuse to
domestic violence against women.

(Blankenhorn 1995: 1)

In countries such as Bangladesh, China, Mexico and Vietnam, millions
of young women were drawn into huge factories, often cutting across
established notions of appropriate behaviour. Across the world, escalat-
ing government budget deficits were addressed through the privatisation of state assets and enterprises, reductions in government spending,
and the scaling back of social programmes and government services.
The gap between the rich and poor continued to grow; it widened
further after the Global Financial Crisis of 2007–2008. The noted US
author Mike Davis (2006) described the world reshaped by free-market
ideologies and their embodiment in structural adjustment programs as a
'Planet of Slums'. Yet while some regions suffered, others prospered,
built as they were around new industries, financial services, cultural
enterprises and tourism. Some neighbourhoods were culturally and
politically homogeneous, others diverse. Being black, gay, feminist or a
union organiser was physically dangerous in some places, nothing special
elsewhere.

The terrorist attacks on the US in September 2001 brought into
focus another characteristic of the twenty-first century: the volatility of
world politics, and the fragility of peace. By 2015, military conflicts –
including those in Afghanistan, Iraq, Bosnia, the Sudan, Chechnya,
Ukraine, Somalia and Syria – produced over 65 million refugees,
asylum-seekers and internally displaced people worldwide (UNHCR
2016). A spate of terrorist attacks on Western countries sharpened
debates about national security, and provided a fertile ground for right-
wing mobilisations against foreigners, Muslims and refugees. Religious
fundamentalism, a movement advocating return to what are regarded as
core sacred texts and traditional patriarchal relations, whether among
Christians, Hindus, Muslims or Jews, deepened social disharmony.

New means of communication were implicated in all these developments: helping to bring together new diaspora, providing the means
of disseminating conservative and radical views, organising dissent and
direct action, building new social movements, and bringing the

suffering of people in war-torn regions into the living rooms of those in safe, well-to-do neighbourhoods. Digital platforms offer individuals new forms of self-expression and communication, but also expose them to threats such as cyber-bullying.

Feminists are among those who have used patriarchy as a conceptual tool for making sense of this rapidly changing world. But so are those debating the merits of war and regime change, far-right groups organising to expel foreigners, fathers reasserting the patriarchal authority they believe is rightfully theirs, fundamentalist Christians trying to bring back God-fearing families, feminist theologians contributing to the creation of a new sphere of respectful public debate, and men trying to forge new forms of non-violent masculinity and pro-feminist spirituality. In a different register, derivatives of patriarchy are employed by scholars analysing forms of patrimonial governance, and those debating the boundaries between appropriate and unjustified paternalist interventions into the lives of vulnerable people.

Feminism and anti-feminism in the twenty-first century

In sketching out the contours of second-wave feminism, Chapters 5 and 6 argued that there was far more diversity than many later accounts claimed. Then and now, local patterns of community activism, neighbourhood organisations, traditions of social analysis and the complexion of academic disciplines and local university departments all made a difference. Surveying women's activism today, many writers stress the same complicated interplay between localities, networks, traditions, organisations (or political and cultural opportunity structures) and different age cohorts (see for example Reger 2012). Against those who mourn or celebrate yet another death of the women's movement, they note that feminists are everywhere and nowhere: rather than marching in the streets, they debate feminist ideas on university campuses and practise feminist principles in workplaces, government organisations, neighbourhoods and local campaigns, and in myriad blogs and online forums. In universities, others note, feminists form a robust and dispersed community of disagreement (Bouchard 2012). Some commentators, at times identifying a third and even a fourth wave of feminism, are optimistic about a resurgence of feminism among young women

(Redfern and Aune 2010). Others are more pessimistic, and draw attention to different forms of 'post-feminism', widespread repudiations of feminist activism, and a powerful anti-feminist backlash.

Those who describe new waves of feminism tend to do so in chronological and generational terms. The third wave, cresting in the 1990s and 2000s, involves the daughters of second-wave feminists. In Britain and the US, Evans notes, third-wave feminists appear keen to avoid engaging in theoretical debates, to the point of being 'anti-academic' – even though they are typically part of a generation who have been exposed to feminism through university curricula (Evans 2015: 221). That said, these young women repudiate what they see as the mistaken assumptions of second-wave feminists: their celebration of universal sisterhood, and their frequent ethnocentrism and racism. Instead, third-wave feminists emphasise the recognition of difference, the fluidity of sexual and gender categories, and the importance of free choice and individual identity. Rather than older forms of collective action, they focus on micropolitics: challenging sexism and misogyny in everyday conversations, in the media and in literature. Even more controversially, some commentators have identified a fourth wave of feminism beginning around 2008, initiated by the next generation of young women, and characterised by extensive use of the internet (Cochrane 2013).

Critics of the wave model of feminism note that feminist activism is far more diverse than the metaphor suggests (see for example Hewitt 2010; Laughlin *et al.* 2011). In any case, feminist uses of the internet – and endorsements of intersectionality – are not confined to the young, but are employed to great effect by those of all ages, including some eminent senior scholars.[1] 'Cyberfeminism' uses social networking sites such as Facebook, Twitter, Instagram, YouTube and Tumblr for debate, writing and organising. In the UK, it includes online campaigns such as The Everyday Sexism Project (http://everydaysexism.com/) and No More Page 3, and websites such as The F Word (www.thefword.org.uk) and The Women's Room (http://thewomensroom.org.uk/); in US many sites are linked to the new Feminist.com (http://feminist.com/).

Whether or not it is associated with a fourth wave of feminism, most commentators agree that uses of the internet introduce a new dynamic into feminist organising. Summarising some of the issues in the US,

Courtney Martin and Vanessa Valenti argue that the current 'war on women' has created the momentum among feminists of a range of ages to fight back. 'Sexism that might have been too subtle to be targeted in a less volatile time', they note, 'is obvious in a climate where women's health, economic security, and sex lives are all under attack'. In turn, 'the explosion of feminist blogs, online organizing (including online petitions), and social media campaigns has transformed the ways in which the movement's most scrappy young entrepreneurs, thought leaders, and grassroots activists think about feminism and discuss the most critical issues of the day' (Martin and Valenti 2012: 5). Some have compared feminist blogs to the consciousness raising which formed an important aspect of second-wave feminism. Others note that online platforms not only help contemporary feminists organise and communicate their ideas, but constitute 'an inexhaustible force continually radicalizing and challenging its institutionalization'. 'While the times we are living in call for social justice movements to embrace decentralization', Martin and Valenti note, 'our technological tools allow coordination among a much broader, more motley collection of organizations and individuals than ever before'. They conclude on a positive note: online feminism has the power to mobilise people – young, old and everyone in between – to take political action on an unprecedented scale at unprecedented speeds. So far this power has mostly been exercised in ad-hoc, reactive (as opposed to proactive), and unsustainable ways, but even so, it has had remarkable effects (Martin 2012: 3).

Kira Cochrane's description of parallel forms of activism in Britain is similarly optimistic about their content and effectiveness. Feminist consciousness in Britain, Cochrane notes, has been forged through the years of hardship following the Global Financial Crisis, and the conservative coalition government responses to it. Many feminist activists have also been politicised by student campaigns against university fees, the wider campaign against cuts to government services, and the Occupy movement. The quick, reactive nature of many of the feminist campaigns cropping up today, she notes, 'reflects the work of activists more generally in a biting world of unemployment and under-employment, workfare, zero-hours contracts, bedroom taxes, damaging rhetoric against immigrants, the disabled and those who need support from the state' (Cochrane 2013). All of this, Cochrane believes, contributes to building a movement capable of taking on structural, systemic problems, economic analyses of women's predicament, and the ways in which neoliberal policies such as the rolling back of the state and low taxes for the rich, have shaped modern inequalities. The movement, she believes, is stronger in its continued endorsement of inter-sectionality, defined as an attempt to elevate and make space for the voices and issues of those who are marginalised, and a framework for recognising how class, race, age, ability, sexuality, gender and other issues combine to affect women's experience of discrimination (see for example Collins and Bilge 2016).

Whatever their age, many contributors to the dispersed world of contemporary vernacular feminism routinely use the term patriarchy to indicate that 'something big and systematic' is going on, and to describe seriously sexist social arrangements. While most feminist scholars employ the concept as an occasional synonym for sexist society, some of those in disciplines such as international politics, theology, literary studies and ecofeminism place it at the core of their analyses. Keenly aware of rapidly changing social circumstances, yet others call for the identification and analysis of new patriarchal bargains. Some busy acti-vists have taken up, in an eclectic fashion, inspiring feminist theorisa-tions of overarching patriarchy by early second-wave authors such as Firestone, Millet, Lerner or French, and use them to explain sexism today. Others, fully aware of scholarly reservations about the concept of patriarchy, call for resurrecting its use when their empirical research uncovers new forms of gender-based discrimination, or shows just how entrenched men's sense of entitlement and violence towards women is in contemporary societies.

In an outstanding paper on feminist criminology in an era of back-lash, for example, Meda Chesney-Lind (2006) notes that in the con-temporary United States, African Americans account for almost half of all incarcerated women. While the imprisonment of African American women grew by 828 per cent between 1986 and 1991, that of white women grew by 241 per cent and of black men by 429 per cent. What is going on, Chesney-Lind suggests, is not just about race or gender, but about both – a sinister synergy that needs to be carefully docu-mented and challenged. In this analysis, she believes, a new, colour-conscious theorisation of patriarchy can play a key role. Such a project, she emphasises, would need to maintain the focus on intersectionality that characterises recent feminist research on gender, race and class. Other feminist criminologists note the increasing use of patriarchy in feminist explanations of gender differences in crime and victimisation, but complain that the concept has been employed as an explanatory wild card that lacks specificity, at times explaining both an *increase* and *decrease* in rates of female crime and delinquency. A more careful operationalising of the concept of patriarchy, they believe, would facilitate future research on gender differences in crime (Ogle and Batton 2009). Yet others confront similar issues, but believe that a critical re-reading of intersectionality rather than patriarchy would not only make possible a focussed critique of mainstream criminology, but encourage an innovative feminist praxis within the discipline (Henne and Troshynski 2013).

In contrast to optimistic portrayals of new forms of feminist activism and scholarship, other commentators are not only sceptical of the claims made for the third and fourth waves, but document young women's repudiations of feminism (see for example Aapola *et al.* 2005; Harris 2004). The British cultural theorist Angela McRobbie (2009), for example, notes that the waves model of feminism homogenises and simplifies a complex history, and retrofits an orderliness and linearity into developments which are far more uneven and complex. More importantly, she argues, the supposed freedoms and actions of third- and fourth-wave feminists in many ways bolster neoliberal, consumer-oriented and anti-feminist social trends. In her broad and spirited critique of post-feminism (a contested term used to indicate that we are now all equal, so feminism is no longer needed, or else a situation where basic feminist demands have been secured, and so a new phase of organising is appropriate) McRobbie characterises recent developments as a 're-instatement of gender hierarchies through new subtle forms of resurgent patriarchal power'. The new sexual contract currently being made available to young women, she argues, involves abandonment of a critique of patriarchy, and amounts to 'resurgent patriarchies and gender retrenchment'.

In her study of repudiation of feminism in Britain and Germany, Christina Scharff (2012; 2014) similarly juxtaposes young women's belief in their capacity to make choices and take responsibility for their own future with the many constraints that they face. Understanding themselves as empowered, liberated, heterosexual individuals, the young women Scharff interviewed saw feminism as a movement of the weak, oppressed and unlovely, incompatible with who they themselves wanted to be. Some, imagining themselves to be free from prejudice, explained that they reject feminism because the second-wave women's movement was white and racist – or else because they visualise feminists as angry, unfeminine, man-hating lesbians (even though they never actually met any such persons). However, most agreed that feminism *is* appropriate to save oppressed Muslim women from patriarchal cultural practices.

Debating fatherhood and reclaiming men's rights

A common theme among young women repudiating feminism is that they no longer need liberation since they now have the same opportunities as men. Accurate or not, a similar assessment has fed into widespread concerns about disenfranchised men and absent fathers and helped to mobilise a wide range of men's rights, fathers' rights and masculinist groups (Blais and Dupuis-Déri 2012; Maddison 1999; Coston and Kimmel 2013).[2] In the US, the sociologist Judith Stacey notes, as part of a national angst over the putative consequences of fatherlessness, men across a broad ideological and cultural spectrum have been rallying to defend fatherhood. This mobilisation includes:

> the mythopoetic men's quest sparked by Robert Bly to commune with paternal spirits in the wilderness; fathers' rights groups contesting for child custody; the Christian Promise Keepers movement crowding massive sports stadiums (and in 1997, the Washington Mall) with men hugging, praying, and testifying to their paternal rebirth; the African-American Million Man March called by Louis Farrahkan in October 1995; the National Center for Fathering founded by Ken Canfield; and the National Fatherhood Initiative that Institute for American Values founder David Blankenhorn spearheaded in concert with an aggressive promotional campaign for his book, *Fatherless America*.
>
> *(Stacey 1998: 67)*

Stacey agrees that contemporary patriarchy is not primarily built around father's dominance of wife and children in the marital home. To name and theorise the diverse forms of male domination we now confront, she concludes, we need to identify a series of alternative new 'post-patriarchal bargains'. As in the past, such arrangements are not standing still, patiently waiting for researchers to name and classify them. Rather, the making of post-patriarchal bargains in different spheres of life is a messy process, keenly contested by activists from all sides of politics.

Patriarchy and bringing up babies

The disputes about absolutism and democracy described in Chapter 3 and the war over the family discussed in Chapters 5 and 6 drew on longstanding debates about the society-wide implications of different models of childrearing. In the twentieth century, these debates were strongly influenced by the work of several male psychologists. In the early 1900s, the New Zealand health reformer and Director of Child Welfare, Truby King, set out to save infants and build character through the application of stern science to motherhood. His firmly held views came to exert enormous influence on the professional advice given to parents in most Western countries. Until the 1950s, mothers and children were terrorised by strict instructions not to pick up or cuddle babies in between four-hourly feeds. A few years later, the pendulum began to swing in the other direction. The American paediatrician Benjamin Spock assured mothers that they knew more than they thought about the needs of their babies, advised them to abandon strict schedules, and advocated more affectionate mothering tailored to individual children. In popular advice literature and policy debates on issues such as childcare and women's paid work, Spock's injunctions were often cited alongside those of the British psychologist John Bowlby. Simplified, Bowlby's attachment theory suggested that in order to thrive, babies needed to have a warm, intimate and ongoing relationship with a primary caregiver, preferably their mother. Conversely, maternal deprivation, such as that caused by women's employment, was likely to lead to long-term social and psychological problems, including affectionless psychopathy, depression and delinquency.

As noted in Chapter 5, in the 1960s and 1970s feminist scholars and activists assembled a vast body of critiques of such views. These ranged from demands for quality, non-sexist education and childcare, equitable access to paid work and recognition of women's unpaid labour, to theorisations of the subconscious sources of patriarchal mentalities, and their reproduction through particular patterns of caring for babies.

King, Spock and Bowlby – and the critiques of their work – were concerned above all with appropriate mothering. By the end of the twentieth century, the focus of public debate was extended to fathers. While feminist theorists such as Chodorow, Dinnerstein and Rubin commended the anti-patriarchal effects of shared parenting, others raised alarm about the seriously flawed adults produced by permissive child-rearing and slack and absent fathers. *The Culture of Narcissism* (1979) written by the American historian and social critic Christopher Lash, for example, was often read as a critique of lax parenting and distant and ineffectual fathers who damaged healthy psychological development, and in particular the formation of a strong superego. Other reformers drew inspiration from Jung's theorisation of a 'collective unconscious' and the core archetypes it contained; many more were inspired by popularisation of such theories by the mythopoetic movement.

Reforming soft males: the mythopoetic movement

In the 1930s, towards the end of his life, the Austrian psychoanalyst Sigmund Freud became convinced that the early events in the history of humanity, including the actual murder of a primeval patriarch, were recapitulated in the psychic life of each individual. Freud's younger colleague, the Swiss psychoanalyst Carl Gustav Jung, articulated a competing theory: all individuals were born with primitive mental frameworks, called 'archetypes', embedded in what he termed the collective unconscious. According to Jung, this collective unconscious (or racial memory) is the biologically based and inherited repository of the universal religious, spiritual and mythological symbols and experiences of humankind. It is built around a series of archetypes, defined as primordial psychic images or patterns, representative of our ancestral experiences, that recur throughout human history in dreams, fantasies, myths and art (Gannon 2008).

Jung's archetypes, as well as a disparate collection of other literary and social science insights, were popularised in Robert Bly's bestseller *Iron John* (1990), and in Robert Moore and Douglas Gillette's *King, Warrior, Magician, Lover* (1990). Contemporary men, Bly argued, became quite good at getting in touch with their feminine side, and caring for partners, children and the environment. But they also became soft, unable to say what they wanted, let alone stick to their resolve. To grow a much needed backbone, these effeminate individuals needed to undertake a scary and difficult journey into the depths of their masculine inner self, preferably in the company of other men and their elder guides. Soon, the quest for healthful male power was enacted in countless gatherings of what came to be called the mythopoetic movement (Bly 1990; Moore and Gillette 1990). Through 'spiritual retreats', encounters with nature, initiation and bonding rituals, the male participants tried to find something primal and heroic; an inner masculinity deeply resonant with themselves as men. Brett McKay (2011), founder of the highly successful men's interest internet magazine *The Art of Manliness*, explained a more secular version of the same project:

> within every man are psychological 'switches' that must be turned on if a man wishes to activate his unique primordial masculine energy. The switches are how you power up the Wild Man within you and overcome the feelings of shiftlessness and male malaise that many men experience these days.

Reclaiming fathers' patriarchal rights

Bly's quest for the wild man is relevant to women's movements – and to discussions of patriarchy – but is not overtly anti-feminist. Many others take sides. Pro-feminist men continue to support egalitarian partnerships with women, and close and caring relations with children.[3] Others energetically oppose the real and imagined gains of the women's movement, and strive to reinvigorate what Connell (1995) called 'hegemonic masculinity'. As Bethany Coston and Michael Kimmel (2013) put it, many angry, straight, white middle-class men feel badly done by individual women or by policies they believe have cheated them. They feel entitled to feel powerful, but they do not. Some groups, often described as men's rights or fathers' rights movements, focus above all on laws and courts dealing with divorce, and the custody and maintenance of children. Many attempt to tackle what they describe as a crisis of fatherhood; some mourn the powerful manliness they feel they have lost, and blame feminists for ruining their lives. The unfair gains of the women's movement and political correctness, some believe, have succeeded in replacing patriarchy by matriarchy that now oppresses men (Blais and Dupuis-Déri 2012: 23, 26) Privileged white men are not the only ones attracted to neo-conservative politics and to men's rights groups; many of those whose livelihoods and communities have been devastated by recent economic restructuring, ineffectual governments and corrupt local officials believe that a radical break with current orthodoxies might lead to a better future.[4] In order to win justice for themselves and improve society, they want to bring back an imagined past of male breadwinner families, devoted wives, obedient children, well-paid masculine jobs and respectful employers and public officials.

As in feminist organising, the internet has played an important role in articulating and disseminating men's grievances, and organising for change (see for example Menzies 2007). The many contributors to groups with substantial web presence, such as Fathers 4 Justice (www.fa thers-4-justice.org), the National Fatherhood Initiative (www.father hood.org/), the National Coalition for Men (http://ncfm.org/) and Voice for Men (www.avoiceformen.com/) do not always agree with each other, present coherent policies, or offer consistent explanations of the problems they identify. However, they are unified in their conviction that feminists have gone too far and, with the connivance of state institutions, robbed them of entitlements and resources that should be rightfully theirs. Family law courts, judges and rulings have come under particularly concerted attack. Forms of activism span the whole spectrum from heartfelt complaints and commentary in online forums, public denunciations of 'the domestic violence industry' and 'feminazis', appeals against court rulings, lawsuits against feminist writers and women's services, proposals for new legislation and protests actions, to bombings of family court buildings and attacks on family court judges, staff, and their families (see for example Summers 2016). Noting the increasing anger of some supporters of the Men's Rights movement in the 1990s, Coston and Kimmel (2013: 376) note that:

the [US] Southern Poverty Law Center, which monitors all sorts of 'hate groups', from paramilitary organizations to Klansmen and other neo-Nazi groups, recently started listing Men's Rights groups in its annual survey of hate, citing what one blogger called their 'virulent misogyny, spreading of false anti-woman propaganda and applauding and even encouraging acts of domestic terrorism'.

* * *

In formulating their claims, many contributors to men's rights forums use the term patriarchy as a general description of the male-dominated world they have lost and wish to reclaim. In his *A Men's Manifesto*, the Australian activist Allan Barron (2001) typically urges his brothers to 'vigorously defend the concept that male domination/patriarchy is part of the natural order of things'. Those who approach similar issues from a Christian standpoint think with patriarchy in a more precise way, and tend to support their claims with specific Biblical passages. Many invest in engendering new forms of manly, muscular Christianity. Others, at times associated with 'men's studies in religion', envision an inclusive, pro-feminist male spirituality (see for example Visser 't Hooft 1982; Gelfer 2009). Many Christian women, often 'driven to despair by the patriarchy and misogyny that reaches out through scripture like a dead hand on women's lives', set out to recast the whole of Christian theology in line with gender-inclusive, non-patriarchal and non-racist principles (Wootton 2016; Carbine 2006; Coakley 2013; Hector 2014). Diverse interpretations of the Christian faith, and the practical implications of different readings of the patriarchal precepts contained in the Bible, have far-reaching social consequences. In the US, for example, around 28 per cent of women and 22 per cent of men attended a church service at least once a week (Mcclendon 2016). Women make up about a third of all seminary students, and between 10 and 20 per cent of clergy, although few appear to head the largest congregations. In 2015, there were around 1,650 very large Protestant 'megachurches' with an average weekly attendance of 2,000 or more persons. Nearly all megachurch pastors were men with considerable personal charisma: single dominant leaders with an authoritative style of preaching and administration, and significant influence on current political debates (Hartford Institute for Religion Research 2016; 2006).

Fundamentalist Protestant and Catholic groups

In attempts to build up their congregations, revitalise Christianity and bring men back to their faith, many churches have drawn extensively on the key themes of both the secular mythopoetic movement and men's rights activism. Although their emphasis in some respects differs, fundamentalist Protestant and Catholic groups alike have taken up notions of archetypes, fatherlessness, wildness, male bonding and the need for initiation among boys in their journey to adulthood. Weak and absent biological fathers – as well as inadequate relationships with God the Father – they believe, produce weak superegos, permissiveness, and emasculated men. In turn, weak men who abdicate their responsibilities to women and are unable to assume a leading patriarchal role in the home perpetuate the crisis of contemporary families. In order to re-establish the authority they have lost and be drawn closer to Christ, soft men have to be hardened by coming closer to a Jungian warrior archetype.

Evangelical Catholic men's ministries are more hesitant about promoting violence and celebrating competitiveness and the pursuit of wealth than their Protestant counterparts, put less emphasis on 'servant leadership', and show more concern with supporting the poor (see for example Rohr and Martos 1992). Fundamentalist evangelical congregations have far more professional resources at their disposal in publicising their message and organising events than do Catholic groups (Hartford Institute for Religion Research 2006). They also tend to embrace warrior images and activities with greater enthusiasm. As one evangelist put it, 'the military version of Jesus has to be re-established if men are to be drawn back to spirituality'. Jesus, depicted 'on a white horse, in a blood-spattered robe, with a sword in His mouth and a rod of iron in His hand' is put forward as 'the ultimate Man. Maximum manhood. The perfect Model' (cited in Gelfer 2009: 51, 55). Military, sporting and hunting metaphors and imagery abound in sermons and online material; major events are staged in sports stadia. To make their places of worship more welcoming, men's evangelical churches use simple accessories such as sawhorses with doors and paint tins with muffins in them. Some congregations combine weekly devotionals with target practice, others hand out full-size swords to all members. Success on the sports field, military service, business prowess and the getting of wealth are celebrated. Men and their sons pose with guns, crossbows and swords, and bond with each other on hunting trips (Gelfer 2009: Ch. 3. See also Bageant 2008). The title of one influential pamphlet is *Raising Boys That Feminists Will Hate* (Giles 2012).

But how are the newly masculine men supposed to rule their wives and children and defer to their pastors? In 1994, a black evangelical pastor from Texas advised men to break the news at home in terms which he would repeat at stadium events to more than 200,000 men who attended that year: 'Sit down with your wife and say something like this: "Honey, I've made a terrible mistake. I've given up my role. I gave up leading this family, and I forced you to take my place. Now, I must reclaim that role." Don't misunderstand what I am saying here', the pastor clarified, 'I'm not suggesting that you ask for your role back. I'm urging you to take it back' (Evans 1994: 79).[5] (On their part, women were advised to 'accept it and live it. Trust it and obey it. Take the orders and follow them' [Weber 1993: 94].)

But while men are frequently literally exhorted to assume – and women to accept – patriarchal authority, this is not portrayed as unbridled individual power. Rather, the aim is 'building a strong marriage and family through love, protection, and biblical values'.[6]

In terms which would resonate with the catechisms of Christian churches in sixteenth- and seventeenth-century Europe, male headship of the family is defined as the responsible exercise of authority delegated by God, interpreted by pastors and priests, and involving serious responsibility for the men's dependents. To explain what this means in more detail, evangelical congregations have adopted the concept of 'servant leadership', a term coined in 1970 by the Quaker management consultant Robert K. Greenleaf. As explained on a typical web page:

> A servant leader seeks to invest himself in the lives of his people so that, as a whole, the church community is challenged to grow to be more like Christ. This is demonstrated in the leader's willingness to give of himself to meet the needs, but not necessarily the wants, of his people. Like a good parent, the true servant leader knows the difference between the needs of his spiritual children and their selfish wants and desires.
>
> *(Got Questions Ministries 2016)*

★ ★ ★

The literal reading of the Bible practised by many evangelical ministries has challenged the long history of humanity and of the Earth which, as described in Chapter 4, inspired nineteenth-century theorisations of ancient patriarchy, and which has since become one of the foundations of the natural sciences. Between 40 and 47 per cent of Americans surveyed over the past three decades now again believe that, as described in the Bible, God created humans in their present form around 10,000 years ago. Among those who attend church weekly, the proportion rises to 69 per cent (Newport 2014). To bring their belief in creation closer to life, they can visit facilities such as the state-of-the-art Creation Museum, which has welcomed over 2.5 million guests since opening in Petersburg, Kentucky, in 2007. There, they can 'experience earth history as God has revealed it in the Bible', learn that all dinosaurs were vegetarian before the fall, cuddle furry creatures in a petting zoo, see how all animals, including the peaceable dinosaurs, fitted into a three-storey ark, and discover new facts about astronomy, biology, anatomy and geology and 'intelligent design' from PhD creation scientists who teach about their subjects of expertise from a biblical world view (*Answers in Genesis* 2016).

In using sacred texts to guide their own behaviour, contribute to public debates and judge others, contemporary Christians continue a tradition stretching back 2,000 years. African American womanist and feminist academic theologians, Roman Catholic cardinals, those practising liberation theology, Quaker pro-refugee and anti-war activists, and gun-toting fundamentalist male ministries and evangelical creationists all take part in reading, translating, explaining, disputing and acting on depictions of patriarchy in the Bible.

The complex and challenging task of interpreting and reforming a monotheist patriarchal religion is shared by Muslims. Soon after its origins in the seventh century CE, Islam became a decentralised religion, with a plurality of theologies. Each of Islam's three main sectarian divisions encompasses diverse and evolving schools of jurisprudence, competing interpretations of the Prophet's actions and words, and a continuing debate about the meaning of sacred texts and their application to everyday life. Today, the complex spectrum of reform movements includes the Malaysian-based Sisters in Islam supporting those who want to be both good Muslims and strong, public women; Iranian Islamic feminists; and radical groups such as ISIS and the Taliban which reject customary practices (including women's rights and entitlements) handed down from generation to generation over the years as heresy, and attempt to put in place an invented version of pristine Islam they claim was practised during the time of the Prophet (Cooke 2005; Göle 1998; 2015). As was the case on many occasions in the past, this complexity tends to be erased in Western commentaries.

Do their women really need saving?

In late 2001, as the US-led invasion of Afghanistan in order to defeat the Taliban got under way, Laura Bush famously justified the war as 'a fight for the rights and dignity of women'. 'Because of our recent military gains', she told listeners in a national radio broadcast, 'women in Afghanistan are no longer imprisoned in their homes. They can listen to music and teach their daughters without fear of punishment' (cited in Abu-Lughod 2002). The US president's wife reiterated widely held views: it was the duty of the chivalrous West to come to the defence of Muslim women viciously oppressed by a foreign, Islamist patriarchal regime. As one feminist commentator summarised it:

> It became painfully clear in 2002, if not before, that the present US government intended to ruthlessly pursue imperial projects identical to those of its colonial predecessors ... Middle Eastern women's status was increasingly exploited by the implacable Washington DC war propaganda machine. 'Saving their women' operated ideologically as a smoke screen for brutal conquest as well as a huge cineplex screen that purported to offer up to public gaze the alleged sufferings of Arab or Muslim women at the hands of their own societies, of their own men. Matters of intimacy as matters of state, as justifications for violent, extra-legal interventions, continue to shape our world.
> *(Clancy-Smith 2006: 182)*

There are now many detailed and persuasive critiques of such portrayals of patriarchal Islam (see for example Kandiyoti 1991; Mohanty *et al.*

2008; Razack 2004). The US anthropologist Lila Abu-Lughod is a particularly influential contributor to such debates (Abu-Lughod 2013). Importantly, she criticises not only misleading portrayals of 'Muslim culture', but reliance on culture-based explanations of women's oppression more broadly. When invited to comment on the USA's role in international conflicts, she notes, experts are asked to give religio-cultural accounts of repressive regimes rather than focus on political and historical explanations of profoundly political issues. To counter such interpretations, Abu-Lughod juxtaposes descriptions of Muslim women in the media to the complexity of people's lives in the Middle East. The resurgence of popular concern about Muslim women's rights after 9/11 in the US, she argues, was strongly influenced by a series of lurid personal accounts such as *A True Story of Life behind the Veil in Saudi Arabia*; *Sold: One Woman's True Account of Modern Slavery*; *My Forbidden Face*; *I Am Nujood, Age 10 and Divorced*; *Without Mercy*; *Burned Alive*; and *Married by Force*, co-written with – or 'as told to' – various ghost writers. In these publications, Abu-Lughod notes, the surprisingly pornographic depictions of sexual violence suffered by individual Muslims helped shape a commonsense understanding of the way patriarchal Islam treats women, and lent passion to the mission of saving women globally. Throughout, the image of the oppressed Muslim woman was contrasted to freely choosing individuals with fulfilling sex lives in the West. Yet domestic violence, poverty, dysfunctional families, bad governments and traumatic change, Abu-Lughod reminds us, are not confined to the Middle East. Indeed, Western countries have contributed to some of the violent events, economic and political upheavals and inequitable trade relations that have brought chaos into Muslim communities in different parts of the world. 'I find it hard to point the finger at patriarchy as the key to women's suffering', Abu-Lughod (2015: 774) concludes.

As a counter to sensationalist accounts of victims of patriarchal Islam, she presents stories of ordinary Muslim women's hardship in which religion is only one aspect of a more complex story. Drawing on thirty years of research in different communities in the Middle East, she shows that poverty and authoritarianism – conditions not unique to the Islamic world, and produced out of global interconnections that implicate the West – are often more decisive. Blinded to the diversity of Muslim women's lives, she notes:

we tend to see our own situation too comfortably. Representing Muslim women as abused makes us forget the violence and oppression in our own midst. Our stereotyping of Muslim women also distracts us from the thornier problem that our own policies and actions in the world help create the (sometimes harsh) conditions in which distant others live. Ultimately, saving Muslim women allows us to ignore the complex entanglements in which we are all implicated and creates a polarization that places feminism only on the side of the West.

(Abu-Lughod 2013)

Debates about banning the wearing of Islamic head coverings tend to draw on the same juxtapositions of enlightened white citizens and brown women oppressed by backward patriarchal regimes. As the Australian Liberal politician Bronwyn Bishop put it in 2005 in an unsuccessful bid to have it outlawed, the veil 'has become the icon, the symbol of the clash of cultures, and it runs much deeper than a piece of cloth'. The successful ban on the wearing of the Islamic headscarf in French schools in 2004, the eminent US historian Joan Scott notes, was justified by French policymakers' concern about 'conspicuous signs' of religious affiliation, and their proclaimed determination to protect women's equality from Islamist patriarchs. Yet behind simple oppositions (including the assumption that patriarchy is a uniquely Islamic phenomenon) were complex developments with urgent political implications. In particular, Scott argues that the ban on wearing headscarves was debated in a climate of growing concern about the loss of national cultural autonomy. Compelled to redefine their national identity within the confines of a newly enlarged Europe, the French mobilised discourses on race, gender and sexuality in relation to a visible, internal Other – in this instance North African Muslim women – as a way to redefine the bounds of appropriate Frenchness (Scott 2007; see also Göle 1996).

Similar issues have been at play in recent attempts to ban the 'burkini', an Australian-invented article of swimwear which conforms to Islamic notions of female modesty. As an Australian commentator noted:

the burkini cannot be stripped of its political context any more than a Ku Klux Klan outfit can be seen as just another hoodie.

> When violent Islamism, with all its misogyny and contempt for secular norms, gathers adherents in the West, the burkini carries an implicit threat.
>
> *(Szego 2016: 18)*

The debate over the burkini was particularly heated in France, where around thirty local authorities banned it in the summer of 2016 on the grounds that it posed a risk of public disorder. The ban was supported by the French premier Manuel Valls, who argued that the burkini was 'not compatible with the values of France and the Republic'. To him, the burkini 'is not a new range of swimwear, a fashion. It is the expression of a political project, a counter-society, based notably on the enslavement of women'. The ban was finally suspended after judges ruled that the 2016 terror attack on the French Riviera city of Nice gave insufficient grounds to justify it (*The Guardian* 2016).

★ ★ ★

Worthy as they are, energetic feminist critiques of simplistic condemnations of Islamic patriarchy do not provide a good guide to action. Certainly, saving brown women from brown men's patriarchy[7] has long been used as a justification for imperialism, domestic discrimination, unjust invasions and wars. Many first- and second-wave feminists not only took over insulting imperial stereotypes of non-Western peoples and their cultures, but helped construct and disseminate them. To make matters worse, careful attention to who has the authority to speak is made more difficult when 'their women' cannot agree among themselves about what they want. All this makes it so complicated that it is tempting to leave 'them' to their own devices. But this does not help young women caught between heavy-handed and often racist interventions from underfunded social services and parents' strategies of family reunification and cultural integrity their daughters strongly suspect will not work out. Neither does it help those caught in war zones or squalid refugee camps. 'How is it possible to acknowledge and confront patriarchal violence within Muslim migrant communities', Sherene Razack (2004) asks, 'without descending into cultural deficit explanations (they are overly patriarchal and inherently uncivilised) and without inviting extraordinary measures of stigmatisation, surveillance and control so increased after the events of September 11, 2001?'

Many feminist critics advocate a respectful politics of cultural recognition (an approach where the reasoning, characteristics and needs of distinct social groups are recognised as equally worthy) in order to deal with such issues. Others argue that cultural relativism (the belief that moral or ethical systems, which vary from culture to culture, are all equally valid and no one system is really 'better' than any other) and the politics of recognition are not enough. The American political theorist Iris Marion Young, for example, argues that what is needed is politics of difference, capable of dealing with the causes and consequences of entrenched privilege:

> it is a significant conceptual and political mistake to reduce group based social movements to movements based in culture, and to suggest that these groups are committed to an essential group identity that they demand to have recognized ... Even more important is achieving an understanding of the way social, economic and political institutions systematically privilege members of some groups, and conceptualizing justifiable remedies for such privilege.
>
> *(Young 1999: 416–417, 420–421)*

Abu-Lughod similarly argues that while cultural relativism is an improvement on ethnocentrism and racism, it is not enough. Saying 'it is their culture and it is not my business to judge or interfere, only to try to understand', she argues, leaves out of the frame of reference a long shared history. What is needed, Abu-Lughod (2013a: 224) suggests, is to look and listen carefully, think hard about the big picture and take responsibility. Rather than seeking to save others, or respectfully leaving them to their own devices, we should use a more egalitarian language of alliances, coalitions and solidarity. This involves working with them in situations that we recognise as always subject to historical transformation, and considering our own larger responsibilities to address the forms of global injustice that are powerful shapers of the worlds in which they find themselves (Abu-Lughod 2013a: 227). 'I do not know how many feminists who felt good about saving Afghan women from the Taliban', she adds, 'are also asking for a global redistribution of wealth or contemplating sacrificing their own consumption radically so that African or Afghan women could have some chance of having what I do believe should be a universal human right'. Importantly, she reiterated, the defence of 'their' human rights should include not only respect for cultural traditions and political preferences, but also a range of basic material safeguards and provisions:

> the right to freedom from the structural violence of global inequality and from the ravages of war, the everyday rights of having enough to eat, having homes for their families in which to live and thrive, having ways to make decent livings so their children can grow, and having the strength and security to work out, within their communities and with whatever alliances they want, how to live a good life, which might very well include changing the ways those communities are organized.
>
> *(Abu-Lughod 2002: 787)*

Many other scholars and activists have addressed the complex task of constructing commonalities among peoples without disrespect to their particular positions and interests. One influential solution is 'dialogical transversal citizenship politics', an approach which provides the 'grammar for democratic conduct'. Such a grammar has to include acknowledgement of one's own positioning(s) while empathising with the ways others' positionings construct their gaze at the world. As Nira Yuval-Davis, director of the Research Centre on Migration, Refugees and Belonging at the University of East London explains it, the discourse of citizenship, of multi-layered memberships in collectivities, with all the rights and responsibilities this involves, became attractive to feminists in different countries in the 1990s because it offered an alternative to the discourse of identity politics that fragmented the women's movement. It offers us a relational contextual tool within which to situate specific campaigns such as on reproductive health, poverty or political participation. It also offers us a particular way of dialogue and coalition building across, at least, three levels of difference – among women in different positionings within one country, among women's networks and NGOs in different countries and among women's movements and the state (Yuval-Davis 1999).

* * *

Interestingly different gender regimes, changing the ways communities are organised, contesting – or strengthening – fathers' patriarchal authority, the promotion of servant leadership by charismatic, authoritarian leaders of evangelical megachurches, building coalitions of likeminded people inside and across national borders, privatising state instrumentalities, challenging or consolidating hereditary claims to political power: all bring to mind new ways of thinking with patriarchy. One promising recent approach to such issues draws on Max Weber's reflections on patrimonialism. While informed by feminist debates about patriarchy, this work makes little explicit reference to them.

Patrimonialism and paternalism in scholarly debates about effective governance

Surveying the world before and after the First World War, in another period of crisis and massive realignment of political power, the noted German sociologist Max Weber developed a range of theoretical and historical insights which later had a profound influence on Western scholarship. Like other fathers of social science, Weber was familiar with the Classics: his doctoral thesis dealt with the agrarian history of ancient Rome. Later in his career, to help him make sense of the rise and fall of great empires and the formation of nation states, Weber juxtaposed two main types of organising governance: patrimonialism and bureaucracy. Patrimonialism, a conceptual kin of patriarchy, allowed Weber to think systematically about political systems in which rulers exerted power on the basis of a combination of familial ties, patron–client relations and personal allegiances, and were bound by few rules and regulations. They were obeyed by those they ruled because their authority was seen as legitimate, underpinned by sacred, immemorial traditions, and cemented by reciprocal obligations towards their subjects.

Patrimonialism, like other key thinking tools developed by Weber, was conceptualised as an ideal type: an abstract model which accentuated the most important aspects of different sorts of social arrangements, but did not accurately describe any one actual historical example of them. As a form of organisation centred on personal networks and the private appropriation of office, patrimonialism stands on the opposite side of the spectrum from another ideal type: rational-legal bureaucracy, defined as involving a written set of regulations, non-hereditary positions, a clear chain of command, and impersonal rules.

Weber's work has often been used to underpin accounts of the gradual development of modern states and bureaucratic organisations, and the more or less peaceful abandonment of traditional ones. Such an approach fits well with accounts of the debates between defenders of absolutism and proponents of social contract (described in Chapter 3), and can relatively easily be translated into feminist theorisations of epochal transitions from one form of patriarchy to another (such as those described in Chapter 6).

The US sociologists Julia Adams and Mounira Charrad (2011; 2015) and their colleagues have recently began using Weber's work on patrimonialism a different way. Rather than progressive stops in a one-way street from tradition to modernity, they argue that patrimonial and bureaucratic forms of governance have coexisted in the past and continue to do so now; new forms of symbiotic relations between hereditary property rights and state institutions keep emerging today. Groups founded on personal relationships of solidarity can congeal around resources that an empire or state cannot provide or control. In some circumstances, they can be more efficient, effective and publicly acceptable than bureaucracies. At other times, they undermine and dissipate the might of great empires or powerful states, are called corruption, and provide the focus of social mobilisation against rulers accused of failing to support and protect their subjects.

In historical work on the Dutch empire, for example, Adams (2005) argues that parcellisation of power between great merchant families, and the patrimonial corporations they established, first fuelled the Dutch Golden Age in the seventeenth century and then contributed to its demise. Even though enough far-sighted contemporaries realised that a measure of centralisation was essential to economic and political survival, they were unable to loosen the patricians' grasp on particular, hereditary powers.

Charrad (2001; 2011) looks at related issues in her work on twentieth-century state formation in Tunisia, Algeria, Morocco and Iraq. In these kin-based societies, she argues, groupings that identify themselves as bound by ties of kinship represent significant political actors at both the political centre and the local level. The different strategies used by a central power towards local patrimonial networks have shaped the process of state building, and resulted in quite different types of modern patrimonial states. In turn, recent popular uprisings in Tunisia and Egypt sought to bring about new political orders and to end the influence of rulers' families in politics, the economy, and social life. They also explicitly targeted hereditary transfers of power that would have codified, in disguise, a reversion to absolutist patrimonial monarchy.

In her work on Lebanon, Suad Joseph (2011) similarly demonstrates how state bureaucracy and reliance on family and kin are fused in the local political system. In a country plagued by a recent history of civil wars, internal fragmentation, political paralysis, and forced movements of populations overdetermined by international conflicts, she shows how people have turned to their families for economic, political and social support. Familial moralities and obligations, she concludes, have borne the burden of the work that the state proved unable to perform. The use of actual or fictive kinship regulates access to state-based services and resources in an intricate web of interpersonal debts and obligations, with the family serving as the final safety net. The political system, in turn, is based on a civic myth of kinship, family allegiances, electoral family politics, and loyalties to political leaders whose sons are assumed to succeed them.

Patrimonial politics are not confined to the past or to non-Western countries. In an example which spans the past and the present, Miller (2015) uses the concept of patrimonialism to think through the implications of the expropriation of indigenous lands in Australia. In Aboriginal societies, she notes, spiritual custodianship of the country, the guardianship and care of particular features of the landscape and sacred objects, was the foundation of a rich cultural system. The wholesale disruption of such relations by whites was gradually consolidated in legislation granting white authorities formal guardianship of all indigenous people for most of their lives. On vast pastoral properties, a form of territorial rule over blacks who 'belonged' to the land was in effect delegated to the propertied 'squatters' who acquired pastoral leases. One of the most pernicious practices of this patrimonial regime was the systematic removal of mixed descent children from their families. The cultural and economic effects of the 'stolen generations', a 1997 Royal Commission noted, meant that entire communities lost, often permanently, their chance to perpetuate themselves in their children. 'This was a primary objective of forcible removals', the Commission concluded, 'and it is the reason they amount to genocide' (Commonwealth of Australia 1997: 187).

Yet another approach to patriarchalism is outlined by Randall Collins (2011). In the contemporary USA (as well as in Russia and Italy), he argues, fictive kinship characterises the patrimonial arrangements that develop in the interstices left untouched by state control, such as in gangs, mafias and crime rings. At the other side of the spectrum, elite groups draw on notions of patrimonial rights in campaigns to reduce or eliminate tax burdens on the rich, use patrimonial resources in seeking election to public office, and employ kin to senior administrative posts when elected. Making a similar case in a South African comedy show, the comedian Trevor Noah compared the then US president-elect Donald Trump to the populist South African leader Jacob Zuma. Among the similarities, Noah explained, were financial conflicts of interest, threats to jail rivals and lashing out at media. Studying South Africa, whose voters 'decided to shake things up and elected a charismatic anti-establishment president', Noah advised *The Daily Show* viewers, was in fact, the best way to prepare for a Donald Trump presidency. Making his case, Noah noted that, until a few years ago, South Africa's economy was 'humming and the country was celebrating its first black president'. In the last few years, he said, the economy has stalled, unemployment spiked, government corruption is rampant, and the country changed 'from a rising power into a troubled state' (Nededog 2016).

★ ★ ★

In both bureaucratic and patrimonial social arrangements, sorting out the precise boundaries between individual (and group) autonomy and the commands of those at different levels of authority is highly contested. Debates and theoretical reflections on these issues often employ the concept of paternalism, another conceptual relative of patriarchy. Where precisely should 'servant leaders' draw the line 'between the needs of their spiritual children and their selfish wants and desires'? To what extent should family law courts delimit men's authority over their wives and children? In medical ethics and practice, should the principle of respect for autonomy, which gives primary decision-making authority to patients, have priority over the principle of beneficence, which gives authority to providers to implement what they regard as sound principles of health care? (see for example Bryant 2002). Should the freedom of citizens be restricted without their consent for the sake of their own good (Bavister-Gould and Matravers 2011)? Should women be compelled to wear – or not to wear – particular forms of head covering? Should people with disabilities be accorded 'the dignity of risk' (Banja 2004; Nay 2002: 33)?

★ ★ ★

This book opened by describing patriarchy as a powerful set of conceptual tools with which social order has been understood, maintained, enforced, contested, adjudicated and dreamt about for over two millennia of Western history. The many unfinished tasks mentioned in this concluding chapter suggest that patriarchy and its conceptual kin will continue serving this function for a long time to come.

Notes

1 Deniz Kandiyoti, Emeritus Professor of Development Studies at the School of Oriental and African Studies at the University of London, for example, makes frequent contributions to the online openDemocracy forum, an independent global media platform publishing up to sixty articles a week and attracting over 8 million visits per year. See for example www.opendemocra cy.net/5050/deniz-kandiyoti/contesting-patriarchy-as-governance-lessons-from-youth-led-activism, accessed 10 October 2016.

2 Among the best-known anti-feminist books are Farrell (1993) and Farrell and Sterba (2008).

3 For an overview of key pro-feminist theorists, see Ashe (2007). For a measured response to fathers' rights claims, see Flood (2003). For an example of 'Anti-sexist, anti-patriarchal, male-positive, pro-feminist Canadian organization that promotes gender justice and equality and nonviolence in human relations', see Men for Change, www.chebucto.ns.ca/CommunitySupport/Men4Change/.

4 Among insightful accounts of community sources of conservative politics are Hochschild (2016), Bageant (2008) and Hedges (2006).

5 The advice is now sent up in a rap song: www.youtube.com/watch?v=
  ZCUAl8r0KQ0, accessed 31 October 2016. For the social effects of such
  advice, see Wilcox (2004).
6 This aim constitutes the fourth of the seven promises at the heart of the
  evangelical Promise Keepers organisation, established in the US in 1990 and
  in several other countries since then. https://promisekeepers.org/about
7 This phrase was used in Gayatri Spivak's famous essay 'Can the Subaltern
  Speak?'

References

Aapola, Sinikka, Marnina Gonick and Anita Harris (2005) *Young Femininity:
    Girlhood, power and social change*. Basingstoke: Macmillan.
Abu-Lughod, Lila (2002) 'Do Muslim Women Really Need Saving? Anthro-
    pological reflections on cultural relativism and its others', *American Anthropologist*
    104(3): 783–790.
Abu-Lughod, Lila (2013a) *Do Muslim Women Need Saving?* Cambridge, MA:
    Harvard University Press.
Abu-Lughod, Lila (2013b) 'Do Muslim Women Need Saving? The Western
    crusade to rescue Muslim women has reduced them to a simplistic stereo-
    type', *Time*, 1 November, accessed 10 October 2016.
Abu-Lughod, Lila (2015) 'Response to the Reviewers', Review symposium,
    Lila Abu-Lughod, *Do Muslim Women Need Saving?*, *Ethnicities* 15(5): 759–777.
Adams, Julia (2005) *The Familial State: Ruling families and merchant capitalism in
    early modern Europe*. Ithaca, NY: Cornell University Press.
Adams, Julia and Mounira Charrad (eds) (2011) *Patrimonial Power in the Modern
    World: The Annals of the American Academy of Political and Social Science, vol. 636*.
    New York: Sage.
Adams, Julia and Mounira M. Charrad (2015) 'Introduction: Old (patrimonial)
    political forms made new', in Mounira M. Charrad and Julia Adams (eds)
    Patrimonial Capitalism and Empire (Political Power and Social Theory, Volume 28).
    New York: Emerald, pp. 1–5.
Answers in Genesis (2016) https://creationmuseum.org/creation-science, accessed
    30 October 2016.
Ashe, Fidelma (2007) *The New Politics of Masculinity: Men, power and resistance*.
    London: Routledge.
Bageant, Joe (2008) *Deer Hunting with Jesus: Dispatches from America's class war*.
    New York: Crown.
Banja, John D. (2004) 'Rehabilitation Medicine', *Encyclopedia of Bioethics*, vol. 4,
    ed. Stephen G. Post. 3rd edn. New York: Macmillan, pp. 2255–2260. Gale
    Virtual Reference Library, accessed 15 November 2016.

Barron, A. J. (2001) *A Men's Manifesto*. Melbourne: Memucan Institute of Men's Studies.

Bavister-Gould, Alex and Matt Matravers (2011) 'Paternalism', *Encyclopedia of Power*, ed. Keith Dowding. Thousand Oaks, CA: Sage, pp. 474–476. Gale Virtual Reference Library, accessed 15 November 2016.

'Bishop Defends Headscarf Comments' (2005) *The Age* (Melbourne), 29 August.

Blais, Melissa and Francis Dupuis-Déri (2012) 'Masculinism and the Antifeminist Countermovement', *Social Movement Studies* 11(1): 21–39.

Blankenhorn, David (1995) *Fatherless America: Confronting our most urgent social problem*. New York: Basic Books.

Bly, Robert (1990) *Iron John: A book about men*. Boston, MA: Addison-Wesley.

Bouchard, Danielle (2012) *A Community of Disagreement: Feminism in the university*. New York: Peter Lang.

Bryant, John (2002) 'Paternalism', *Encyclopedia of Public Health*, vol. 3, ed. Lester Breslow, New York: Macmillan, p. 892. Gale Virtual Reference Library, accessed 15 November 2016.

Carbine, Rosemary P. (2006) 'Ekklesial Work: Toward a feminist public theology', *Harvard Theological Review* 99(4): 433–455.

Charrad, Mounira (2001) *States and Women's Rights: The making of postcolonial Tunisia, Algeria, and Morocco*. Berkeley: University of California Press.

Charrad, Mounira (2011) 'Central and Local Patrimonialism: State-building in kin-based societies', in J. Adams and M. Charrad (eds) *Patrimonial Power in the Modern World: The Annals of the American Academy of Political and Social Science, vol. 636*. New York: Sage.

Chesney-Lind, Meda (2006) 'Patriarchy, Crime, and Justice: Feminist criminology in an era of backlash', *Feminist Criminology* 1(1): 6–26.

Clancy-Smith, Julia (2006) 'The Intimate, the Familial, and the Local in Transnational Histories of Gender', *Journal of Women's History* 18(2): 174–183.

Coakley, Sarah (2013) *God, Sexuality and the Self: An essay 'On the Trinity'*. Cambridge: Cambridge University Press.

Cochrane, Kira (2013) *All the Rebel Women: The rise of the fourth wave of feminism*. Guardian Shorts Originals eBook. https://www.theguardian.com/world/2013/dec/10/fourth-wave-feminism-rebel-women.

Collins, Patricia Hill and Sirma Bilge (2016) *Intersectionality*. Oxford: Polity Press.

Collins, Randall (2011) 'Patrimonial Alliances and Failures of State Penetration: A historical dynamic of crime, corruption, gangs, and mafias', in J. Adams and M. Charrad (eds) *Patrimonial Power in the Modern World: The Annals of the American Academy of Political and Social Science, vol. 636*. New York: Sage.

Commonwealth of Australia, Human Rights and Equal Opportunity Commission (1997) *Bringing them Home: Report of the National Inquiry into the*

Separation of Aboriginal and Torres Strait Islander Children from Their Families. Sydney: HREOC.

Connell, R. W. (1995) *Masculinities*. Sydney: Allen and Unwin.

Cooke, Miriam (2005) 'Islamic Feminism', *New Dictionary of the History of Ideas*, vol. 2, ed. Maryanne Cline Horowitz. New York: Scribner's, pp. 817–820. Gale Virtual Reference Library, accessed 31 October 2016.

Coston, Bethany and Michael Kimmel (2013) 'White Men as the New Victims: Reverse discrimination cases and the Men's Rights Movement', *Nevada Law Journal* 13(2): 368–385.

Davis, Mike (2006) *Planet of Slums*. London: Verso.

Evans, Elizabeth (2015) *The Politics of Third Wave: Feminisms, neoliberalism, intersectionality and the state in Britain and the US*. Basingstoke and New York: Palgrave Macmillan.

Evans, Tony (1994) 'Spiritual Purity', in Al Janssen (ed.) *Seven Promises of a Promise Keeper*. Colorado Springs, CO: Focus on the Family, p. 79.

Farrell, Warren (1993) *The Myth of Male Power: Why men are the disposable sex*. New York: Simon and Schuster.

Farrell, Warren and James P. Sterba (2008) *Does Feminism Discriminate Against Men?* New York and Oxford: Oxford University Press.

Flood, Michael (2003) 'Fatherhood and Fatherlessness'. The Australia Institute, Discussion paper #59, Canberra, November.

Gannon, Thomas (2008) 'Jung, Carl (1875–1961)', *Encyclopedia of Counseling Vol. 2: Personal and Emotional Counseling*, ed. Frederick Leong, Elizabeth Altmaier and Brian Johnson. Thousand Oaks, CA: Sage, pp. 667–668. Gale Virtual Reference Library, accessed 26 October 2016.

Gelfer, Joseph (2009) *Numen, Old Men: Contemporary masculine spiritualities and the problem of patriarchy*. London: Equinox Publishing.

Giles, Doug (2012) *Raising Boys That Feminists Will Hate*, White Feather Press, whitefeatherpress.com

Göle, Nilüfer (1996) *The Forbidden Modern: Civilisation and veiling*. Ann Arbor: University of Michigan Press.

Göle, Nilüfer (1998) 'Istanbul to Hong Kong: Notes on non-Western modernities', *New Perspectives Quarterly* 15(2): 40–43.

Göle, Nilüfer (2015) *Islam and Secularity: The future of Europe's public sphere*. Durham, NC: Duke University Press.

Got Questions Ministries (2016) 'Question: "What is servant leadership?"' http s://gotquestions.org/servant-leadership.html, accessed 30 October 2016.

Harris, Anita (2004) *Future Girl: Young women in the twenty-first century*. New York: Routledge.

Hartford Institute for Religion Research (2006) 'Megachurches'. Hartford, CT: Hartford Seminary, http://hirr.hartsem.edu/index.html, accessed 7 November 2016.

Hartford Institute for Religion Research (2016) 'Fast Facts about American Religion'. Hartford, CT: Hartford Seminary, http://hirr.hartsem.edu/index. html, accessed 7 November 2016.

Hector, Kevin W. (2014) 'Trinity, Ascesis, and Culture: Contextualizing Coakley's *God, Sexuality, and the Self*', *Modern Theology* 30(1): 561–566.

Hedges, Chris (2006) *American Fascists: The Christian right and the war on America.* New York: The Free Press.

Henne, Kathryn and Emily Troshynski (2013) 'Mapping the Margins of Intersectionality: Criminological possibilities in a transnational world', *Theoretical Criminology* 17(4): 455–473.

Hewitt, Nancy (ed.) (2010) *No Permanent Waves: Recasting histories of US feminism.* New Brunswick, NJ: Rutgers University Press.

Hochschild, Arlie Russell (2016) *Strangers in Their Own Land: Anger and mourning on the American right.* New York: The New Press.

Joseph, Suad (2011) 'Political Familism in Lebanon', in J. Adams and M. Charrad (eds) *Patrimonial Power in the Modern World: The Annals of the American Academy of Political and Social Science, vol. 636.* New York: Sage.

Kandiyoti, Deniz (ed.) (1991) *Women, Islam and the State.* Philadelphia, PA: Temple University Press.

Lash, Christopher (1979) *The Culture of Narcissism.* New York: Norton.

Laughlin, Kathleen A., Julie Gallagher and Dorothy Sue Cobble (2011) 'Is It Time to Jump Ship? Historians rethink the waves metaphor', *Feminist Formations* 22(1): 76–135.

Maddison, Sarah (1999) 'Private Men, Public Anger: The men's rights movement in Australia', *Journal of Interdisciplinary Gender Studies* 4(2): 39–52.

Martin, Courtney E. (2012) 'Introduction: Online revolution', in Courtney E. Martin and Vanessa Valenti, *#FemFuture: Online feminism.* New Feminist Solutions series, vol. 8. New York: Barnard Center for Research on Women, Columbia University.

Martin, Courtney E. and Vanessa Valenti (2012) *#FemFuture: Online feminism.* New Feminist Solutions series, vol. 8. New York: Barnard Center for Research on Women, Columbia University.

Mcclendon, David (2016) 'Gender Gap in Religious Service Attendance Has Narrowed in U.S', Pew Research Center, www.pewresearch.org/fact-tank/ 2016/05/13/gender-gap-in-religious-service-attendance-has-narrowed-in-u-s/, accessed 30 October 2016.

McKay, Brett (2011) 'The Four Archetypes of the Mature Masculine: Introduction', 31 July. www.artofmanliness.com/2011/07/31/king-warrior-ma gician-lover-introduction/, accessed 29 October 2016.

McRobbie, Angela (2009) *The Aftermath of Feminism: Gender, culture and social change.* London: Sage.

Menzies, Robert (2007) 'Virtual Backlash: Representation of men's "rights" and feminist "wrongs" in cyberspace', in Susan Boyd, *Reaction and Resistance: Feminism, law, and social change*. Vancouver: University of British Columbia Press, pp. 65–97.

Messner, Michael (1997) *Politics of Masculinities: Men in movements*. Thousand Oaks, CA: Sage.

Miller, Pavla (2015) 'Antipodean Patrimonialism? Squattocracy, democracy and land rights in Australia', in Mounira M. Charrad and Julia Adams (eds) *Patrimonial Capitalism and Empire (Political Power and Social Theory, Volume 28)*. New York: Emerald, pp. 131–156.

Mohanty, Chandra, Minnie Pratt and Robin Riley (2008) *Feminism and War: Confronting U.S. imperialism*. London: Zed Books.

Moore, Robert and Douglas Gillette (1990) *King, Warrior, Magician, Lover: Rediscovering the archetypes of the mature masculine*. San Francisco, CA: HarperCollins.

Nay, R. (2002) 'The Dignity of Risk', *Australian Nursing Journal* 9(9): 33.

Nededog, Jethro (2016) 'Trevor Noah compares Trump to South Africa's scandalous president', 17 November, *Business Insider Australia*. www.busi nessinsider.com.au/trevor-noah-donald-trump-south-african-president-jacob -zuma-2016-11?r=US&IR=T, accessed 25 November 2016.

Newport, Frank (2014) 'In U.S., 42% Believe Creationist View of Human Origins', *Politics*, 2 June. www.gallup.com/poll/170822/believe-creatio nist-view-human-origins.aspx, accessed 25 October 2016.

Ogle, Robbin and Candice Batton (2009) 'Revisiting Patriarchy: Its conceptualization and operationalization in criminology', *Critical Criminology* 17: 159–182.

Razack, Sherene (2004) 'Imperilled Muslim Women, Dangerous Muslim Men and Civilised Europeans: Legal and social responses to forced marriages', *Feminist Legal Studies* 12(2): 129–174.

Redfern, Catherine and Kristin Aune (2010) *Reclaiming the F-word: The new feminist movement*. London: Zed Books.

Reger, Jo (2012) *Everywhere and Nowhere: Contemporary feminism in the United States*. New York: Oxford University Press.

Rohr, Richard and Joseph Martos (1992) *The Wild Man's Journey: Reflections of male spirituality*. Cincinnati, OH: St. Anthony Messenger Press.

Scharff, Christina (2012) *Repudiating Feminism: Young women in a neoliberal world*. Farnham: Ashgate.

Scharff, Christina (2014) 'Schröder versus Schwarzer? Analysing the discursive terrain of media debates about feminism', *Feminist Media Studies* 14(5): 837–852.

Scott, Joan Wallach (2007) *The Politics of the Veil*. Princeton, NJ: Princeton University Press.

Stacey, Judith (1998) 'What Comes After Patriarchy? Comparative reflections on gender and power in a "post-patriarchal" age', *Radical History Review* 71 (Spring): 63–70.

Summers, Anne (2016) 'Domestic Violence Industry Bashing', *The Age* (Melbourne), 3 November, p. 30. http://monumentaustralia.org.au/themes/culture/crime/display/22716-family-court-tragedy;   www.dailytelegraph.com.au/rendezview/miranda-devine-answers-her-critics/news-story/45ab5055e5 59f22606db617c62322ca9

Szego, Julie (2016) 'Burkini's Veiled Threat', *The Age* (Melbourne), 11 September, p. 18.

The Guardian (2016) 'Burkini Ban Suspended by Nice Court, Dismissing Claim of Public Order Risk', 2 September, https://www.theguardian.com/world/2016/sep/02/burkini-ban-suspended-nice-court-france, accessed 17 October 2016.

UNHCR (United Nations High Commissioner for Refugees) (2016) *Global Trends: Forced displacement in 2015*. www.unhcr.org/576408cd7.pdf, accessed 19 October 2016.

Visser 't Hooft, Willem (1982) *The Fatherhood of God in an Age of Emancipation*. Geneva: World Council of Churches.

Weber, Stu (1993) *Tender Warrior: God's intention for a man*. Colorado Springs, CO: Multnomah Books.

Wilcox, W. Bradford (2004) *Soft Patriarchs, New Men: How Christianity shapes fathers and husbands*. Chicago, IL: University of Chicago Press.

Wootton, Janet (2016) 'Editorial', *Feminist Theology* 25(1): 3–7.

Young, Iris Marion (1999) 'Ruling Norms and the Politics of Difference: A comment on Seyla Benhabib', *Yale Journal of Criticism* 12(2): 415–421.

Yuval-Davis, Nira (1999) 'The "Multi-Layered Citizen": Citizenship in the age of glocalization', *International Feminist Journal of Politics* 1(1): 119–136.

INDEX

of 41–2, 76, 80 n3, 84–5, 106,
109; laws 12, 16, 18; contract 101;
see also primitive marriage; rape in
marriage
Martin, Courtney 123
Marx, Karl 13, 20n3, 42–5, 64, 68, 79
Marxism 57, 61–2, 65–7, 70–6, 78
masculinist groups 126
masters and servants 3, 8, 16
mater familias 48
materialist feminism 65, 76, 78, 97
maternal deprivation 127
maternalism 108
matriarchy 7, 30, 35–7, 45, 47–9, 51,
69–71, 111, 130 primitive 70
matrilineal 35, 39, 43, 45, 70, 80n3
matrilocal 70, 80n3
McCarthyism 66
McKay, Brett 129
McLennan, John Ferguson 37–40,
46–7
McRobbie, Angela 125
means of production 45, 72
means of reproduction 67
megachurches 131, 141
men's rights 65, 126, 130–32
mental discipline 14
mentality 60, 78, 128
metaphors 2, 94, 132
Mexico 120
Middle East 88, 135–6
militarism 91, 104
Miller, Henry 55
Miller, Pavla 106, 143
Millett, Kate 55–60, 62, 80n1, 96
Mills, Charles 102
misogyny 59, 122, 131, 138
Mitchell, Juliet 51, 61–4, 72, 89, 96,
100–1, 109
modernisation 87, 105
modernity 3, 142
Moi, Toril 95
monarch 23–5, 143
monogamy 35, 38, 41–2, 48
Moore, Robert 129
Morgan, Lewis Henry 40–47, 59

Moses 50, 62, 101
mother right 35, 45
motherhood 57–8, 127
mothering 66, 77, 127–8
Moynihan, Daniel 111
Muslim 15, 88, 120, 126, 134–8
mythopoetic 51, 126, 128–9, 132
myths 35–7, 56, 128, 143

nature 2, 24, 33, 96, 98–9, 129;
human 13, 31, 36, 39
Négritude 111
New England 58, 105
New Left 53, 61, 85, 108
New Right see political Right
New Testament 3, 15–16, 30
New Zealand 9, 61, 65, 127
Noah, Trevor 144

O'Brien, Mary 67
Occupy movement 123
Oedipal 50, 62–3, 65, 90, 97, 101–2,
108
Oedipus Rex 49
Old Testament 3, 6, 15–16, 20, 30,
33, 65
ordination 16, 19, 60
Oriental 37, 112n2, 145n1
Ortner, Sherry B. 2, 71, 86
Other, the 95, 137

Palaeolithic era 68
Pandects 8, 12, 43
parenting 66, 128
Parmar, Pratibha 87–8, 109
pastors 25, 131, 133
Pateman, Carole 27, 100–2, 106
pater patriae 24
paterfamilias 8–9, 34, 48, *see also*
Roman patriarchs
paternalism 141, 144
patria potestas 34, 40
patriarchal authority 121, 132–3, 141;
bargains 88, 124, 127; concepts 4,
96, 100–1, 131; culture 34, 37, 72,
95–6, 99, 111, 126, 138; family 2,

Rome 6–7, 12–13, 34, 36, 43, 70, 141
Rosaldo, Michelle Zimbalist 69, 71, 80n5
Rothenberg, Paula 90, 92–3
Rousseau, Jean Jacques 26–7
Rubin, Gayle 61, 63–5, 69, 89, 128
Rupp, Leila 84, 92

sacred sites 87, 143
Sanderson, Robert 24
Satan 20
savage 31–2, 38, 41, 45
Scharff, Christina 85, 125–6
Schiller, Friedrich von 31–2
Scotland 10, 37
Scott, Joan 89–90, 137
Seccombe, Wally 105–6
self-mastery 26–7, 106
Seneca 40
serfdom 46
servant leadership 132–3, 141, 144
servant 11, 16, 24–5, 27, 28n2, 74, 105
Sewell, William H. jnr 85–6
sex-gender system 65, 75
sexism 54, 62, 65, 122–4
sex-right 101
sex-role 56–7, 65, 95, 108, 111, 133; see also gender role 97–98
sexual 35, 58–9, 77; abuse 18, 120, 136; asymmetry 68, 71; categories 122; contract 100, 102, 125; desire 63; difference 62, 96; dominance 63, 90; equality 71; intercourse 35–7, 101; needs 65; oppression 73; politics 55, 66, 74; revolution 57; system 64, 67, 71, 77, 79
sexuality 35, 64–5, 67, 72, 74, 77–8, 92, 106, 108, 124, 137; see also homosexuality; heterosexuality
Sisters in Islam 135
slaves 8, 11, 40, 45, 48, 57, 111, 138
slavery 32, 35, 46, 136
social contract see contract, social

social movements 53–4, 66, 78–9, 85–6, 120, 139
socialisation 56–7, 60, 62, 72–3, 95, 108
socialism 46–7, 105
socialist 46–47, 49, 55, 65, 71, 85; feminist 61, 66, 72–3, 78; scholarship 68
Somalia 120
Sophocles 49–50
South Africa 144
southern theory 86
spirituality 19, 37, 69, 121, 131–2
Spivak, Gayatri 90, 146n8
Spock, Benjamin 127–8
Stacey, Judith 91, 105, 109, 126–7
Stalin 28n1
status 13, 35, 46, 56–8, 69, 71–2, 77, 135
Stewart, Mary 99
stolen generations 144
structural adjustment programmes 120
structuralist analyses 85–6
Sudan 120
suicide 58
superstructure 57
suttee see widow burning
Syria 7, 120
System, the 53–5, 59–60, 63, 67, 71, 77, 104

Tacitus 32
Taliban 135, 139
Taylor, Barbara 73, 112n1
technology 36, 41–2, 59, 67–8, 123
theologian 16, 18–19, 59, 121, 134
theology 19, 59–60, 124, 131, 134; see also liberation theology
total social division of labour 104
totem 5n1, 51, 62, 101
transhistorical 60, 71, 84, 88, 93, 101, 104, 107
Tribonian 7, 15
Trivedi, Parita 109–10

Trump, Donald 144
tuberculosis 37, 47
Tyson, Lois 97–8

UK 55, 65, 109, 119, 122
Ukraine 120
unconscious, the 61–3, 72; collective
 50, 128
United Nations 88
United States 9, 55, 59, 66–7,
 87, 89, 91, 98–9, 109, 111,
 119–20, 122, 124, 126, 131,
 135–6, 144
University 9–10, 12, 15, 87, 90–2,
 121–3; Columbia 55; Harvard 18;
 Sverdlovsk 46, of Berlin 13, 42–3;
 of Bologna 16; of Bonn 42; of East
 London 140; of Fribourg 59; of
 Jena 42; of London 112n2, 145n1;
 of Vienna 49

Valenti, Vanessa 123
veil 57, 88, 136–7
vernacular 9, 17, 20n2, 95, 124
Vietnam 53, 105, 120
Vogel, Lise 66

wage labour 46
wages for housework 73
Walby, Sylvia 106–7
Warren, Karen 99
Washington DC 126, 135
Weber, Max 79, 141–2
welfare 85, 105, 108, 110
white dividend 85
widow burning 57, 60, 88
women's movement *see* feminism;
 social movements
women's dependence on men 19;
 equality 40, 47, 49, 74, 137; influence
 36; liberation 54, 62, 66–7, 93, 108;
 movements 4, 37, 47, 55, 66, 71, 75;
 oppression 4, 45, 54, 66–7, 69, 73–4,
 76, 89, 92, 96, 136; position 46–7,
 72–3; property legislation 8, 11;
 qualifications 54; rights 8, 40, 54, 85,
 135–6; role 62; studies 18, 84, 91–2;
 subordination 70–2, 78, 92–3

Young, Iris Marian 139
Yuval-Davis, Nira 140

Zuma, Jacob 144